MW00997579

WHEN

How the Emotional Health of Leaders Impact
Everything & Everyone They **Lead**

THE
HEAD

DR. KHAALIDA FORBES

HURTS

Copyright © 2023 by Khaalida T. Forbes
All rights reserved. This book or any portion thereof may not be reproduced or used in any manner whatsoever without the express written permission of the publisher except for the use of brief quotations in a book review.

Limits of Liability and Disclaimer of Warranty

The author and publisher shall not be liable for your misuse of this material. This book is strictly for informational purposes. The purpose of this book is to educate. The author and publisher do not guarantee anyone following these techniques, suggestions, tips, ideas, or strategies will become successful. The author and publisher shall have neither liability nor responsibility to anyone with respect to any loss or damage caused, or alleged to be caused, directly or indirectly by the information contained in this book. Views expressed in this publication do not necessarily reflect the views of the publisher.

Printed in the United States of America
Keen Vision Publishing, LLC
www.publishwithkvp.com
ISBN: 978-1-955316-72-9

Eternal God,
Thank you that you see, know, and in your perfect timing you will always restore. We find peace and safety with you.

Thank you for every soul that has trusted me with their stories. I give you this work as a first fruits offering of what's to come.

CONTENTS

FOREWORD

Psalms 23:5b says, "*You anoint my head with oil; my cup runs over.*" What a profound statement from a man multilayered in philosophy, experience, and expectation. This prophetic psalm was written through the crucible of experience that led to a boy shepherding in the field, being anointed as king over all of Israel. From defending a few sheep from the occasional wolf, lion, or bear to ruling millions of people, David represents the complexities of leadership and the profound implications of one whose cup had run dry yet had to keep leading.

The anointing is not always indicative of a full cup. The anointing rests on individuals, marking them as God-sanctioned, and then graces them to function in a particular calling. We often assume that the anointing on a leader transcends any issue that he/she might face. On its face, that is a true statement; however, their cups can run dry, leading to dangerous practices. It's the daily dance of ministering dry that often leads to breakdown.

If a car engine runs out of oil, that engine will lock up, rendering a once useful implement of transportation inert and no better than a paperweight.

When one has run out of oil, functioning properly becomes a task of gargantuan proportions. The dry leader is in trouble, and all who follow them are at risk because the oil flows down from the head. In the state of a dry cup, the leader is at risk of faltering, falling, and or imminent failure. Dr. Khaalida Forbes has penned a treatise that addresses the ills of a leader whose emotional oil is on the verge of running out. The dichotomy of a firm and tender touch, while simultaneously applying a healing salve to the minds of leaders, is necessary in a day when functioning failures are plenty and easily found if one were to peruse social media for just a few moments. *When The Head Hurts* captures the essence of how healing can begin for, as Henri Nouwen calls it, the Wounded Healer. Dr. Forbes masterfully navigates leaders through the obstacle course in our minds while carefully leading us to a place of discovering the issues and healthily managing recovery when we, the heads, the leaders, are hurting.

Acknowledging our brokenness is the first step toward the hope of healing our brokenness. If we never decide that being made whole is a necessity, we will simply drive the car, hoping that today is not the day when the oil completely runs out. Like the engine, there are always warning signs before failure occurs. As leaders, we cannot simply wash the car to hide the ticking time bomb under the hood. After acknowledgment, the decision must be made to allow a licensed, trained mechanic to look under the hood. Dr. Khaalida Forbes is well versed and competent in her field, housing the expertise to help leaders find their way back to where their cups are replenished, and their saucers are holding the overflow.

When The Head Hurts gives tactical answers and sage wisdom to leaders who find it difficult to delegate running headlong into potential burnout. This book will help leaders differentiate between when they are powerful leaders and when they, too, are sheep needing a shepherd. Within these pages, leaders will be guided to confront their own brokenness and unaddressed trauma while also receiving tools for a path of recovery and replenishment. You will see that rest is a godly mandate that is often ignored, and lastly, you'll receive a detailed understanding of the ethics of spiritual leading that ensures the maintenance of the leader's health while guiding others to health.

I pray that this book will nourish your mind, nurture your curiosity about healthy leading, and nudge you into the chair of a therapist who can help you navigate life. Read this book, knowing that healing has already begun.

Bishop Jason Nelson

INTRODUCTION

It's not by happenstance that you find yourself reading this book. You've been led to read it because you are a leader, and we know that leaders are, if nothing else, givers. You are always giving of your knowledge, gifts, talents, time, care, resources, energy, and finances. You are expected to always be available to pour, guide, and direct. As a leader, you must be able to oversee what is happening now while simultaneously projecting into the future and returning to the present, all in order to provide people with the steps needed to journey ahead. *What a dance.*

When there is a need, people look to you for solutions. When there is confusion, people look to you for clarity. When there is doubt, people look to you for reassurance. When there are questions, people look to you for answers. Amid crisis, you are expected to navigate people through, no matter how treacherous the terrains. Great are the burdens of a leader, especially those chosen to lead within an ecclesial context. Those who follow your lead often have no clue of the full load on your shoulders. They are unaware that you often give of yourself even when there is nothing left to give. They don't know that you extend energy to care for them that you often don't have to care for yourself. Sadly, because you hold the title of leader, many never perceive that you would have a need.

If you were honest, you would have to admit that the people are not completely to blame. After all, your selflessness and fortitude make leading look easy. Since assuming the role of leader, you've probably placed unhealthy expectations upon yourself.

Think about it for a moment.

You are always consuming with the immediate thought that you have a mandate to pour out what you've just consumed. You sit in spaces, hear a profound concept, and immediately think about those you lead or someone you know who would benefit from hearing it. In your mind, you think, "*Wow, Sean really needs to hear this. Let me take notes for him.*" Or, "*The members of my ministry need to hear this. Let me tweet this out for them. Better yet, let me jump on my social media pages and record this because people need this in their lives!*" All the while neglecting that as a leader, you need to fully receive it, too, and often, you need to receive it first. You are supposed to be the first partaker. Did you ever considered that God orchestrated you to be in that space, on that day, at that specific time, because He wanted to talk *to you*? Has your constant serving of others caused you to forget how to *sit and eat* from God's table for yourself?

When you hear about devastation or catastrophe on CNN, FOX NEWS, or your local news station, you immediately think, "*I need to create a statement so that the people know I understand and I'm here to guide them through this.*" All the while forsaking to take a moment and think about how the news has impacted your mind, heart, and spirit. You don't know how you truly feel because you don't give yourself the space to truly feel. Have you forgotten that what goes on in the world impacts you as well? Have you forgotten that your feelings are just as valid as the feelings of those you lead? Have you forgotten that what you feel deserves just as much attention and care?

At the onset of difficult challenges or transitions within your organization, is your first thought to ensure the well-being and clarity of the people? While that is important, do you ever stop to think about how the difficult experience is affecting you? After so many years of caring for others, has it become difficult to remember that you also...

felt the loss...
felt the grief...
felt the fear...
felt the uncertainty?

Yes, leader, you are gifted, anointed, and educated...
but *you are also human.*

Yes, leader, you are called to the nations...
but *you also need to be refreshed and refueled.*

This book is not for anyone else before it's for YOU! It's not for your friends who are leaders. It's not for your family who are leaders. It's not for your staff. This book was designed specifically with **YOU** in mind. These pages are...

- *your safe space* to catch your breath
- *your chance* to investigate how you got to this place
- *your opportunity* to finally begin to heal

God orchestrated you to be reading this book in this season of your life because He wants to talk to you. Through the years, you have counseled, supported, and encouraged countless people through their seasons of hurt and pain. Don't you deserve to pause and give attention to your hurts? Yes, the organization is important. *But so are you.*

The truth of the matter is the organization you lead can go no further than your level of internal wellness. If you want to take your organization to higher heights and make the influence God has called you to make in the earth, you must believe that you deserve the care you've given others.

Take a moment and think about a vehicle. It is designed to transport you from point A to point B. However, in order to ensure that the vehicle does its job well, you must have it checked out and maintained regularly. In addition to helping it run well, regular maintenance ensures the vehicle's longevity. If you live in an area that experiences tough winters, you know all too well how vital it is to have your vehicle checked out. Winter seasons come with snow, ice, sludge, and harsh temperatures, all of which can impact the functionality and life span of a car. In the same manner, you, as a leader, endure winters. You've endured seasons of what appeared to be barrenness. You've experienced heartache, pain, and abuse. You've smiled through cold, heartless rumors and gossip about you. What a shame it would be to give our vehicles more care after difficult winters than we give ourselves. What a shame it would be to help others through their life winters while, year after year, ignoring the frostbite we've acquired from our own. Leaders, you deserve this opportunity to heal.

You may have difficulty accepting that you need this time to heal because you perceive that you are not hurting. Leader, understand that pain manifests in various ways. May I humbly suggest that...

You're not angry...*you're hurting.*
You're not frustrated...*you're hurting.*
You're not defensive...*you're hurting.*
You're not controlling...*you're hurting.*
You're not manipulative...*you're just hurting.*

Every trauma, every disappointment, and every verbal, emotional, physical, sexual, and spiritual misuse and abuse you've experienced, all the lies told about you, each person that left when they promised to stay, from birth up to the very moment you find yourself reading this book, it all hurt you in ways that you haven't allowed yourself to be consciously aware of. But the truth is, you were hurt and are most likely still hurting. You never got the examination, diagnostic, and prescription you needed and deserved. You've never been able to be the patient, and for that, I am deeply sorry. But I do have good news for you...

The Doctor will see you now!

My heart goes out to that little child, that young adolescent, to that twenty-something young adult.

What age were you when **IT** *happened?*
What age were you when **IT** *didn't happen?*

As you are now chronologically an adult, I want to respectfully suggest that you're physically older, but you may still be stuck in the age and developmental stage where **IT** happened. So my questions are simply...

How old are you?
What is your **emotional** *age?*
Are you old enough **emotionally** *to pastor?*
Are you old enough **emotionally** *to be a CEO?*
Are you old enough **emotionally** *to handle the weight of a million-dollar building program?*
Are you old enough **emotionally** *to lead hundreds and thousands of people who, themselves, are of various emotional ages?*

These questions are vital for a leader to ponder on and truthfully answer. The reality is, we simply cannot fix that which we are unwilling to face. At the end of the day, you can teach and preach out of what you know, *but you can only lead out of who you are*. When the **HEAD** hurts, the **BODY** hurts. The body's health is directly connected to the health of the head. The two are inseparable.

> "*And He is the head of the body, the church, who is the beginning, the firstborn from the dead, that in all things He may have the preeminence.*"
>
> **COLOSSIANS 1:18**

As the head of the church, whatever Christ does impacts the church as His body. He is seated in heavenly places; therefore, we are seated in heavenly places. Christ is victorious; therefore, we are victorious. Everything Christ did was so that His church, His body could reap the benefits of being in covenant with God. The Bible also makes it clear in Psalms 133:2 that the oil flows down from the head and onto the body. What does this all mean for you, leader? **Everything you do or refuse to do will impact those you lead.**

Will you take a moment to consider that perhaps you aren't seeing the growth you desire in your organization because you have not grown? Is it possible that *congregants are still blind* to what ails them because *you are blind* to your ailments? Is it possible that those who follow you are passive-aggressive, anxious, distrusting, or bound in repetitive cycles because of what's hidden in the corridors of *your heart*? Again, when the **HEAD** hurts, the **BODY** hurts.

Take
a
deep
breath....

It can be difficult to process that as a leader, your selflessness is hurting your organization more than it is helping it. It can be disappointing to realize that years of putting your healing on the backseat for the sake of progressing the organization may have actually contributed to the stunting of its maturity. It's hard to realize that every time you sacrificed rest to move the organization ahead, you only took the organization a few steps back. Not only does your emotional and mental well-being impact the progression of the organization, but it also affects the health of your organization. May I suggest that your pain may be impacting how you see God and portray Him to His people? What if you are engaging the scriptures from your place of brokenness? What if the way you perceive the issues of the sheep is impacted by the trauma you've experienced?

Who is your hurt hurting? Your family? Friends? Staff? Members? Those who follow you from afar? Oftentimes, these people are afraid to tell you that you're hurting them. They love you, care for you, and depend on you (spiritually, emotionally, and, for some, financially). They often don't have the words to articulate the impact that your emotional state has on their lives, or they simply don't have the courage to speak that level of truth to you because of your position of power.

The goal of this book is not to condemn you. I want you to know, leader, that they don't know what I know. *I know that you are in no way intentionally hurting them.* However, what I also know is that hurt people unconsciously hurt other people.

When The Head Hurts is your opportunity to stop, assess, breathe, and heal. I pray this book will be God's way of reaching out to you in your internal distress. God has seen what you experienced, and God has heard your cries. Let God use this book in this season as one of many tools to rescue you from your emotional Egypt so that He can bring you into a season of peace, stability, and overflowing joy. Let me pray for you...

Eternal God,

I pray for everyone you have divinely orchestrated to read this book. You are the author of these pages because you desire to speak to your children. You want them to know that regardless of how big they've become, they're still your child. Father, you know every story, every incident, every misuse and abuse. You know when it happened, where it happened, and how long it lasted. You know every internal emotional fracture and every broken place within them. All I humbly ask of you is that you reveal to each reader the importance of their past's impact on their present and future. Allow this to be a sacred season wherein they can truly see the need for healing. From this book, guide each one toward the genesis of a healing journey that is tailor-made just for them. Allow this book to be the seed that opens their mind, heart, and spirit to their need to receive your healing balm. Lastly, heal those our hurts have wounded, and ultimately usher us all into the beauty, peace, and strength that comes from the fountain of holy wellness.

In Jesus' Name, Amen, It Is So.

Chapter One

DO YOU WANT TO BE MADE WELL?

The current climate of the church of the living God finds itself in the middle of an internal audit. The light of exposure has been turned on, and what previously couldn't be seen is now plainly and painfully visible. Private challenges have become public. The very things we thought were hidden (situations, struggles, sins, and strongholds; proclivities, passions, perversions, and pride; desires, dis-eases, dysfunctions, and demons) have now been laid bare before us all. Mainstream print, television, and social media have had a field day reporting *dark* situations that were never intended to see the *light* of day. And just when we think we've heard it all, another unfortunate situation surfaces. If that one wasn't damaging enough, here comes yet another one.

Why now? Why are things being exposed so suddenly within the body of Christ? Why are so many ministry leaders at the center of ridicule, scandal, and strife? The reality for the 21st-century church, however difficult to digest, is that perhaps our insides are infected, causing swelling that we, at times, presumably and incorrectly labeled as growth. That which is internally unclean has now oozed out and is creating quite an external mess. It is a quandary so great that there is no longer room for it beneath the proverbial carpet under which we have, for so long, attempted to contain it. It has spilled out for the world to see, and we can no longer afford to ignore it.

For years, we have endeavored to clean the mess by placing great emphasis on the congregation's mental, emotional, and spiritual well-being. Leaders worldwide have gone to great lengths to ensure congregations can access resources to aid their internal emotional strife. We've hosted mental health webinars, labored to create mental health sermon series, employed mental health professionals, and worked altar calls of deliverance until we were voiceless. Church leaders have searched high and low for solutions focused on assessing congregants, hoping to offer concrete methods of healing and transformation. Yet, the state of the church remains the same. Despite our many efforts, church leaders still see clouds of emotional and mental dysfunction looming about the width of their sanctuaries.

However, in recent years, there has been a necessary shift in the direction of the concern of Christian communities. With a painfully high increase of church leaders committing suicide, which started in 2013, leaders being the center of consistent scandal, and even walking away from ministry altogether after only a couple of years, it seems that, perhaps, church leaders have been trying to solve the dilemma within the church with a focus on the wrong variable. While traditionally, the focus was solely on congregant care, the church appears to be shifting to look at the care of those who lead our congregants. After years of thinking that if a church was experiencing challenges, it was due to the congregants experiencing challenges, we have finally shifted our perspective to see the biggest variable in the equation. We are finally at the point of accepting the difficult reality that many of the church's current crises do not necessarily stem from the pew *but from the pulpit.*

It is said that in order to destroy an army, focus should be placed on crippling, tainting, or altogether removing the army's general. Likewise, if you want to destroy the body, it would prove quite successful to start with the head. It is no secret that the adversary desires to destroy the church. Therefore, many are finally awakening to the fact that Satan's greatest tactic is to strike those in positions of ministerial leadership, to put it plainly, senior lead pastors. Now that we find ourselves fully aware of the enemy's strategy, it is no longer acceptable for those who profess to be called to lead the body of Christ to ignore their role in the dysfunction therein.

> *If you want to destroy the body, it would prove successful to start with the head.*

Before you close this book and decide it is not for you, I invite you to read further. I come in love and peace. I can now say that I'm fully aware of the weight of the role of the senior leader. I offer this book not as an attack on Christian leaders but as a safe space where you can peer into the corridors of your soul and partner with God to resolve any issues hiding within.

The truth is that you have been waiting for someone to acknowledge your pain. If you would be honest, you can admit that you have been desperate for a breakthrough in the emotional components of your life. You have been waiting for someone to recognize that though you exist physically when it comes to your emotions, you have been in a comatose-like state for possibly decades. You've desired someone to have empathy that you have been through a lot, and the truth is, you are emotionally exhausted. Though you would never let the words escape from your lips, sometimes not even in prayer, you have been desperate for a change, desperate for the same healing you've walked others through, desperate for someone to see you, the real you, beyond the title, call, and anointing. The weight upon the shoulders of a senior leader is greater than that of any other middle management role. Your members, deacons, ministry leaders, and staff don't understand, but I do,

Truthfully, you've been waiting for someone to acknowledge your pain.

and I penned this book to let you know that I see you and God cares.

....You've been serving faithfully, but your soul is wounded. *I see you.*

....You are physically on your post, but your mind is tormented daily. *I see you.*

....You haven't slept well in years. *I see you.*

....You are pouring into God's people, but you still get flashbacks of being touched inappropriately. *I see you.*

....You are believing God to do miracles, signs, and wonders for the families in the church you lead while your home is fractured and in disarray. *I see you.*

....You are declaring financial freedom over the faithful tithers, but you have been sowing, too, and are barely making ends meet. *I see you.*

....Despite what your life has been like, the mistakes you've made, the trauma you've endured, and the pain you've suffered in silence, *I SEE YOU.*

And I believe you CAN have a soul-prospering life and be the healthy leader God created YOU to be.

I wrote this book to speak over and through the lies your trauma whispers about your identity. This resource is not designed to offend or belittle you but to remind you of everything the pain of your past caused you to forget about who God says you are. This book is the alarm and the permission you have been waiting for to **stop, breathe, and heal.** I pray that you will eulogize the days of serving everyone to the expense of sacrificing, neglecting, and dishonoring the needs of your soul, all in the name of ministry. I pray that you will realize that it is, in fact, not sacrifice — it is a sin against the sacredness of your humanity.

Leader, just as we labor, fight, and pour so that others can experience breakthroughs, we sometimes need someone willing to do the same for us. This book is my God-inspired attempt to do just that for you. Reading this book won't always be comfortable, but if you press in and through, I promise to provide you with the tools you need to get to the root of your issues. **So, take a deep breath.**

No, really.

Stop.

Breathe.

Now, let's keep digging.

THE CONNECTION BETWEEN YOUR EMOTIONAL HEALTH & SPIRITUAL MATURITY

When you (the head of your church's organizational structure) refuse to be honest about the state of your emotional health, the church will experience many casualties of war. Yes, you have sermons to write, couples to counsel, meetings to lead, and decisions to make. However, to carry out your assignment as God has designed you to, you must be emotionally well.

Your unwillingness to become aware of and monitor your emotional state impacts your ability to lead well. The overall health of what God has commissioned you to oversee requires you to understand the connection between your emotional health and spiritual maturity.

The key to successful spiritual leadership has much more to do with your internal life than your expertise, gifts, or experience. If you assumed that the growth of your church depended on how well your sermons moved the hearts of the biggest givers in your church, you were wrong. If you spent time tirelessly trying to perfect your whoop and find the best organist in town to back you while you're preaching, you've wasted your efforts. If you searched high and low for a popular worship leader who could draw a crowd and add to your congregation, you had it all wrong. Real, healthy growth (remember, we know the difference between swelling and growing) begins with you prioritizing your emotional well-being. YOU must be emotionally healthy in order to build a healthy church.

> *The health of a church depends on the emotional health and spiritual maturity of its leader.*

What I find beautifully ironic is the many leaders who have now realized how vital it is to be in shape physically. Across the landscape of Christendom, you see ministry leaders challenging and holding each other accountable for weekly physical exercise. So we have no problem finding a gym and even a personal trainer, however, not many leaders are running to a *therapist's couch*. Though we can easily see the need for therapy for the congregation, leaders sometimes struggle to see that they also need a therapist. This is mostly because our emotional well-being is invisible. As visionaries, we naturally spend a lot of time focused on what can be outwardly seen.

We can see the size of the congregation.

We can see the state of the finances.

We can see the turnouts at events.

However, our emotional state isn't as visible or tangible. I submit to you that though it may not be visible, it is extremely vital.

No, you cannot touch anxiety, but it is real, and you must deal with it. You cannot sit down and have a face-to-face conversation with rejection, but that does not stop it from negatively impacting your life. You know the scriptures, leader. We battle in warfare with an invisible adversary. Though it can't be seen with natural eyes, we can still feel the impact of the fight. 2 Corinthians 4:18 (KJV) offers us this wisdom, "*So we fix our eyes not on what is seen, but on what is unseen, since what is seen is temporary, but what is unseen is eternal.*" As you read this book, I challenge you to fight to see the impact of the invisible. I want to challenge you to prioritize your emotional health, even though no one can outwardly see it. You may not get a pat on the back from Brother

Joe saying, "*Hey, Pastor, your smile is especially genuine today. Have you been healing?*" Nevertheless, spending time healing emotionally is the best decision you can ever make because, over time, your soul, your family, and those you serve will thank you.

Even though we battle with our emotions internally, if we don't heal properly, the side effects will manifest externally. Yes, leader, what cannot be seen will eventually come into view. Time and time again, we have witnessed leaders become the object of scrutiny as their private life made its premiere on social media outlets. We become susceptible to this kind of public shame, not because we have not covered our tracks well enough... but because there were tracks to cover in the first place. Many reckless choices stem not just from temptations but from unaddressed inner turmoil. It's time for your emotional well-being to be addressed so that more lives don't become casualties of your inner wars.

> *Many reckless choices stem not just from temptation, but unaddressed inner turmoil.*

> "*Beloved, I pray that you may prosper in all things and be in health, just as your soul prospers.*"
>
> 3 John 1:1

God desires you to be emotionally well. He cares about the emotional state of the leaders He's called to steward His branches of Zion. But how can you be a devout soldier on the battlefield for the Lord while internally fighting your demons alone? It's excruciatingly difficult to play your part in the fight for souls with a wounded soul. I know what some of the ecclesial leaders of past generations did, but God is not requiring you to lead and preach broken. You don't have to bleed while you lead. God is not opposed to you taking the time you need to sit and deal with everything affecting you emotionally. In this season, God is demanding that you do just that. Here's why, leader...

The underworld does its bidding through our open wounds. You already know this because you have taught your congregation about open doors of rejection, offense, rebellion, and abandonment and how they taint our view of God, others, and ourselves. Just as you can see how those spirits impact your congregation's ability to see properly, those same spirits also impact your ability to see and hear God correctly concerning those you are helping to see Him. God wants you to deal with your emotions so the underworld can lose its grip on you. Thus losing its hold on those God has appointed you to shepherd.

It's difficult to play your part in the fight for souls with a wounded soul.

Stop.

Breathe.

Let's continue.

Sometimes, leader, you hear God through your rejection, abandonment, pain, and frustrations. Contrary to popular belief, your gift doesn't make you immune to the underworld working through your emotional deficiencies. It is very possible to prophesy addresses and social security numbers but still be emotionally unwell. You can operate in the power of deliverance so strongly that demons flee just by you being on the premises, but that does not negate the fact that you are housing them, too. You can lay hands on the sick, and they experience full healing, all while you are in need of a doctor. Your gifts do not give you immunity from emotional sickness.

Your gifts do not give you immunity from emotional sickness.

Many of you reading this book know you are emotionally unwell. You know that despite looking the part, you haven't *felt* the part in years. When the sermon is over and the day ends, you can't wait to get in the car to remove the smile you've forced all day. The years of heartache you have experienced in and out of ministry have affected you so much that you don't even know if you still believe the God you preach about. Your heart has become so calloused that you struggle to stay attentive in meetings and barely trust those seated around the table. You know that what you need now, more than ever, is some time to breathe, be real with yourself, and deal with the years of trauma that have brought you to your current state. However, you won't take the time you need because you are afraid to go on a real sabbatical. You are afraid to admit to your pastor friends that you are hurting. After all, the world knows you to be *that* preacher, and you cannot dare taint your reputation by disappearing for a few months to heal. So, you continue with the game of charades. You tell yourself, "*But the church needs me.*" Leader, you **NEED** you.

Trust me, I understand. The idea of stepping away from the church you feel belongs to you (we'll get to that later) is difficult. May I humbly submit to you that as you continue this path of self-neglect, you are doing more damage to *your* church than helping. It's not the worship leader, your elders, or even the tension you feel from other pastors in your city. **Your church is not where it could be because you are not emotionally where you should be.** It may seem unfair to place that responsibility on you, but as a leader, it is the truth. As the head, the body grows according to your growth. When you ignore the signs suggesting you may be emotionally unhealthy, you are more vulnerable to falling into actions that do not align with the core values of the faith you profess. With that in mind, let's discuss some of the traps many emotionally unwell leaders fall into and a few indicators that a leader is not emotionally well.

Breathe in.........

Breathe out.......

SIGNS THAT A LEADER MAY BE EMOTIONALLY UNWELL

1. Selfish Ambition *Devoted to or caring only for oneself; concerned primarily with one's own interests, benefits, welfare, etc., regardless of others. Characterized by or manifesting concern or care only for oneself; selfish motives.*

When a leader is emotionally sick, it is difficult for them to seek God's will over their own. They will struggle to discern the difference between God's voice and the voice of their frustration, insecurity, abandonment, etc. Leader, it is possible that the goals you have for your church aren't godly. It's possible that the building renovation isn't God's plan, but your desire to appease the little child in you who grew up in extreme lack and misfortune and prove your worth through outward success. It's possible that this ministry you want to develop isn't God's idea but your attempt to fill the void of genuine friendships in your life. Yes, leader, it's possible that God has not signed off on the conference, but it's a plan you've devised to no longer feel like a *small-town pastor* amongst your *big-time associates*. Again, there is a direct connection between your emotions and how well you hear God.

> *There is a direct connection between your emotions and how well you hear God.*

Selfish ambition will cause you to spend time, money, resources, and energy on things God does not have His hand on. But wellness is available. *Leader, do you want to be well?*

2. **Extreme Feelings of Entitlement** *The belief that one inherently deserves privileges or special treatment.*

The enemy has a field day in the minds of leaders who fall into the pit of entitlement. Entitlement will cause a leader to believe they should know *everything* happening with *their* members and be a part of every decision they make for their lives. They feel dishonored when *their* members move, marry, take a new job, or do anything without consulting them. Entitled leaders believe they own the souls of *their* congregants. Some tell themselves it is just their desire to cover them well, but that's rarely the underlying truth. These types of leaders want full knowledge without full care. But wellness is available. *Leader, do you want to be well?*

Entitled leaders believe they own the souls of congregants.

3. **Narcissism** *Selfishness, a lack of empathy, and a need for admiration characterizing a personality type. Extreme Self-centeredness arises from failure to distinguish the self from external objects. Excessive interest in or admiration of oneself.*

A great deal of leaders suffer from narcissism and

don't even know it. Their wounds have convinced them that it is more important for the people to know about them than God. Their narcissism has convinced them that they are deserving of God's glory, honor, and attention. They, directly and indirectly, hold expectations of those around them to regard and engage them in a kingly manner. This posture causes them to veer off in their sermons that should point the listeners to Christ, but the direction points to them. Their church staff spends more of their week strategizing and planning for the leader's outside entrepreneurial ventures than they do on the missions of their local church body. Why? *Because everything is about THEM!* What's fascinating about these leaders is that they're unaware they behave in this manner. Usually, only a front-facing crisis or threat of major loss can awaken them to their mindset and behavior. But wellness is available. *Leader, do you want to be well?*

Have your wounds convinced you that it is more important for people to know about you than God?

4. Insecurity *Lack of confidence or assurance; self-doubt.*

An insecure leader can't see a conference flyer or event without wondering why they weren't invited to speak. They attend conferences and feel a way when the host doesn't invite them to sit on the stage. Whenever insecure leaders go somewhere, they throw their Pastor/Prophet/Apostle/Dr. title around, hoping that it shifts the way they're treated. When they don't get the response they desire, they are usually offended. It's not honor that they are seeking; it's purely attention. A leader who struggles with insecurity wouldn't dare bring in someone more proficient than they are in an area. They are too concerned with the individual walking away with *their* members. And if they bring in someone who is exceptionally proficient, they will quickly regret that choice as they watch them operate and mistreat the individual in the hopes of breaking them down. But wellness is available. *Leader, do you want to be well?*

5. SEXUAL SCANDAL *A scandal (a circumstance or action that offends propriety or established moral conceptions or disgraces those associated with it.) involving allegations or information about possibly immoral sexual activities being made public.*

Both single and married leaders can be susceptible to sexual scandals when emotionally unwell. Yes, the hot and heavy meet-up they have once a month with someone who's not their spouse is often an indication, not of unrestrained desire, but of a soul that may be deeply wounded. Many leaders often use sex that is biblically unsanctioned by God as a numbing tool to escape the volume of their inner turmoil. The biological children your wife and your congregation know about prove that you need to seek help. The mere fact of having to carry such massive secrets can, in and of itself, bring great torment to a leader's soul. If you find yourself in the middle or on the brink of a sexual impropriety scandal, know that there is help and hope. Leaders, you can recover. But before crafting a beautiful confession and apology for social media, apologize to yourself for refusing to take the time you needed to have been well enough to have made a different choice. Then, **HEAL.** Heal so you can stand before God's people with a clean conscience and clean hands. Heal so you can honor the call God has placed on your life. Wellness is available. *Leader, do you want to be well?*

> *Many leaders use biblically unsanctioned sex as a numbing tool to escape the volume of their inner turmoil.*

6. DICTATORSHIP *Having absolute power; a person who does whatever they desire with no consideration of other's feelings, desires, needs, or opinions.*

Leaders who fall into dictatorship soon find themselves surrounded by *yes* men and women. These leaders don't have congregants, staffers, or laymen who respect them. Everyone around them is afraid of them. People walk on eggshells around them for fear of misstepping, speaking, and/or disagreeing. Leaders who fall into dictatorship don't develop those entrusted to their care because they fear competing with them. Leaders who struggle in this area must be careful, especially in this new era and with this new generation. Gone are the days when individuals will choose to remain in unhealthy environments that produce fear and uncertainty. Dictatorship is a clear way to ensure you'll end up building alone. Leaders need helping hands, extra sets of eyes, and other perspectives. You need people around you who have the courage to respectfully tell you the **TRUTH.** Unfortunately, unless you heal those emotional wounds, you'll never be secure enough to value others and what they, too, bring to the table. But wellness is available. *Leader, do you want to be well?*

Deep breath in...

Deep breath out...

Alright. Let's wrap up this chapter.

Coming face to face with the areas within you that require change or growth can feel uncomfortable. We often view discomfort as harmful, thus avoiding it at all costs. However, I want to suggest that your avoidance has gotten too expensive, and you can no longer afford to foot the bill. If reading any of the previous descriptions made you feel uneasy, understand that your uneasiness is only a sign that God wants to heal you in that area. It's a *divine invitation*, not a *carnal degradation*. The only way to deal with your emotional health challenges is to go through them, not avoid them. You can't go around... *you must go through*. Ignoring the symptoms will not bring about the prescription, and ignoring the prescription won't bring the cure. Sometimes, healing will hurt first. Sometimes, you have to open the wound to do surgery on the wound. But I promise you that temporary hurt is worth a lifetime of wellness.

Despite what you have encountered, if you would be honest with yourself and get the help you need, you can be the leader God called you to be. The enemy uses tactics to keep leaders emotionally entrapped. He knows that if he can keep you entangled in trauma, you will remain stagnant, and so will the church God has appointed you to lead. Can you imagine hundreds and thousands of people being held hostage simply because the leader they have chosen refuses to get well. I often reflect on January of 2011, when, while seated in a morning session at United Theological Seminary, Rev. Dr. Floyd Flake confirmed what I knew to be truth when he said, "In order to save the church, we must deal with the emotional health of church leaders."

I know you probably think this is a lot, and it is. But I'm on a mission to help you get free. **This is about you.** This is your chance to face the truth and grow into the leader God has called you to be. When we are confronted with and accept the truth, it is easier to embrace the idea of close and continual examination of self as we lead and examine others. This book is simply being offered as a first step in you attending to your emotional health.

As you try to figure out how you will get through this book, remember to *breathe*, pace yourself, and grace yourself. We must remember that change often demands process. The first step of that process is **awareness.** We cannot fix what we are unwilling to face. It is imperative that you realize how your emotional health is impacting the emotional health of the body. It is imperative that you realize how your emotional health is impacting your quality of life. But most importantly, it is imperative that you realize how your emotional health is impacting your relationship with the God of your salvation. It is not until these connections are faced, accepted, understood, and embraced that you will be open to receiving the emotional support you need and deserve.

THE QUESTION

> "*Sometime later, Jesus went up to Jerusalem for one of the Jewish festivals. Now, there is in Jerusalem near the Sheep Gate a pool, which in Aramaic is called Bethesda and which is surrounded by five covered colonnades. Here, a great number of disabled people used to lie—the blind, the lame, the paralyzed. One who was there had been an invalid for thirty-eight years. When Jesus saw him lying there and learned that he had been in this condition for a long time, he asked him, "Do you want to get well?"*"
>
> **JOHN 5:1-5**

In this very familiar passage of scripture, we find Jesus on his way to a festival. On his journey, he is interrupted, not by the multitude of people swarming around the pool of Bethesda but by one lame man, in particular. It wasn't that Jesus wasn't concerned about the other people's healing, but Jesus saw something else going on with this man other than his physical inability. There was something *deeper* keeping him from accessing healing.

Jesus poses the question, "*Do you want to be made well?*" To the naked eye, Jesus' question could be seen as insensitive. Of course, the man wanted to be made well. Honestly, who would want to spend the rest of their life ill? Jesus didn't ask this question to offend the man. I believe Jesus' intent was to invite him to evaluate his emotional state and its impact on his ability to truly have the faith and subsequent tenacity for wellness. Jesus wanted the lame man to take accountability for his wholeness.

The Bible tells us that this man had been in this state for 38 years. This lets us know that he found a way to live his life while wounded. He found a way to conform his life to his brokenness. When Jesus comes along and asks this question, he offers the man an opportunity to finally separate from his sickness.

You know this biblical story, leaders. The lame man never answered Jesus' question. He made an excuse as to why he couldn't previously get well. But what I love about this story is that Jesus totally ignores the excuse and commands the man to get up. The Bible tells us that immediately after Jesus' command, the man was made well, took up his bed, and walked.

Before I pose this question to you again, I want

you to take a moment to reflect. How much is your handicap impacting you? How much energy have you put into conforming your life to your ailment? How much have you lost? What opportunities have you missed because you reduced your life to your trauma effects? We can spend so many years in unwell states that we become accustomed to it. We find ways to make the uncomfortable comfortable.

Whether we're dealing with blindness... an inability to see the potential in ourselves or others, being trapped in darkness longing for the clarity that comes from the light, or consistently tripping over obstacles that clarity of sight could have prevented.....

BLIND *Unable to see. Lacking perception, awareness, or discernment.*

Whether we're lame... with the very things or people charged to hold us up, leaving us limp and unable to step forward, no sure foundation.....

LAME *Unable to walk, weak or ineffectual.*

Or....

Whether we're paralyzed or living with the extremities to function, our emotions leave us immobile, stagnant, and unable to gain traction. Our lives stuck on repeat for forward movement is a distant memory......

PARALYZED *Unable to move, helpless stoppage, inactivity*

Either of these three can leave the best of us feeling

like the worst of us. But the beauty is that Jesus sees you in your current immobile state, just as he saw that man at the pool of Bethesda, and he's posing the same question to you today, "*Do you want to get well?*"

If you do, turn the page. I'll meet you in Chapter Two.

Chapter Two

POLISHED PAIN

WE WEAR THE MASK

WE wear the mask that grins and lies,
It hides our cheeks and shades our eyes,—
This debt we pay to human guile;
With torn and bleeding hearts we smile,
And mouth with myriad subtleties.
Why should the world be over-wise,
In counting all our tears and sighs?
Nay, let them only see us, while
We wear the mask.
We smile, but, O great Christ, our cries
To thee from tortured souls arise.
We sing, but oh the clay is vile
Beneath our feet, and long the mile;
But let the world dream otherwise,
We wear the mask!

PAUL LAURENCE DUNBAR (1872-1906)

2013 started with an alarming number of senior leaders committing suicide. After many of these tragedies were mourned, it was later revealed that these leaders suffered silently from mental and emotional health concerns. How painful is it to realize that someone who stood behind the sacred desk, week in and week out, encouraging, uplifting, and declaring life over bowed heads and broken hearts, secretly battled seeing value in their own life? How dreadful is it to know that leaders who held counseling sessions and talked others off the ledge felt alone atop their own cliff? How devastating is it that those who casted devils out of others were so traumatized by their own demons that the only freedom they saw was death?

Upon the announcement of many of these tragedies, social media was filled with other senior leaders showing their support, sharing their condolences, and, of course, encouraging leaders not to suffer in silence. Many held discussions in which they interrogated, "*Why did these leaders stay silent? How is it that no one around them saw the signs that something was wrong?*" And, understandably so. In many of these cases, days before those leaders chose to take their lives, pictures were captured of them wearing the biggest smiles. Looking at those photos put people in deeper bouts of confusion, wondering, "*But they looked perfectly fine.*"

However, as a senior leader yourself, it should not be difficult to understand how they could've appeared to be perfectly fine outwardly while inwardly they were not. Though you may have never considered suicide, for years, many of you reading this book have worn the very same mask. You know the one I'm referring to. It's the face of excitement you put on, though you barely got rest the night before because you spent hours wrestling with trauma flashbacks. It's the poker face you put on when you walk through the sanctuary doors, even though you had a serious argument with your spouse moments earlier and are still emotionally flustered. It's the face of joy you wear even though you just got the most unpleasant text message from a family member moments before you entered the meeting.

Despite what has happened throughout the week, when it is time to stand before the people, leaders across the world reach into their bags and pull out their good and faithful masks to hide the horrors, cover the casualties, and disguise the disappointments. It's the mask that makes everyone else feel safe, secure, and supported except for the wearer. It allows volunteers and staff to think the leader is listening and interested, even though their minds couldn't be further away from what is being discussed.

> *Many leaders wear masks to hide the horrors, cover the casualties, and disguise the disappointments.*

Sadly, for many leaders, masks aren't just something they use temporarily to press through trying moments. Some have been wearing masks for years. You see, leader, masks go beyond the false facial expressions and misleading body language you employ. Masks also come in the form of other items you may employ to cover pain, trauma, heartbreak, abandonment, and rejection. Very often, your desire to always look your best, wear the best clothes, buy the best shoes, have the nicest car, and obtain academic prowess isn't for the sake of your enjoyment or progression. If you were truthful, you could admit that you've used those things to cover up the years of issues you have tucked away in the corridors of your heart. In your mind, you believe that if you can just look strong, sound competent, and appear whole, no one will ever notice that your soul is unraveling.

Take a deep breath in.
Now release it *slowly.*
We are going to get through this together.

Once again...
Take a deep breath in...
and release....

PRIVATE/ INNER STRUGGLES

Many of our life struggles aren't occurring because of what's happening outside of us, as much as what's happening INSIDE of us. Even though we know that we are struggling, we often aren't honest with ourselves about those struggles. Therefore, we aren't honest with others about our struggles. We feel so guilty and weighed down by our secret struggles that we unconsciously attempt to:

- Deny
- Displace
- Numb (Use of Alcohol, drugs, sexual promiscuity, excessive shopping, overeating, gambling, overworking, fixated parenting)

This is where the mask comes in. We wear masks to hide the things we're struggling with privately. When people ask us how we're doing, we say things like, "I'm too blessed to be stressed," when we know that we are stressed out of our minds. Ironically, God sent someone across our path to ask us how we're doing, not just as a common courtesy/ salutation but because they care. However, because we are not honest with them, we've missed the opportunities to get the care and attention we desperately need. The sad reality is that in addition to being dishonest with others, we are also dishonest with ourselves. We've worn the mask so often that we no longer know our authentic emotional state.

Our life struggles don't occur because of what's happening outside of us but rather, what's happening INSIDE of us.

AM I WEARING A MASK?

Everyone's masks look different depending on what they are trying to cover up, who they are trying to hide the truth from, and the platform they desire to obtain or maintain. Let's discuss a few ways you can be sure that you are wearing a mask...

You avoid God by serving God.

This is most seen in leaders who require themselves to be the first one at the church and the last to leave. You've ordained and trained over 50 leaders but refuse to allow them to do their jobs and fulfill their positions. You tell yourself (and others) that you run ragged doing everything because you "love the Lord and the church." You just want to hear God say, "Well done!" when you reach the gates, right? Wrong. Your busyness isn't an attempt to serve God or His people. It's a cover-up. The truth is, you know that if you sit still too long, the Holy Spirit will begin to whisper to you about you. You're frantically serving God to prevent hearing God!

You embrace positive emotions but flee from any negative feelings that surface.

If there's a conversation about the amazing things occurring at the church, you want to be front and center of that conversation. You enjoy high moments when things are going great, and everyone is happy. However, when conflict and confrontations arise, you pass that off to your team. Since behaviors bleed, you also carry this behavior over into your family and other relationships. When alone, you think about all the positive things you feel. However, when anything negative pops into your mind about your life, accomplishments, or the lack thereof, or anything concerning connected to you, you instantly pack those feelings away. You tell yourself you are optimistic and looking at the glass half full rather than half empty, *but that isn't true.* The truth is, you're avoiding negative emotions because you fear what they will uncover. You're afraid of unpleasant emotions surfacing and what you will have to do to address them. Your outlook on life is unrealistic. You fail to realize that God also speaks to you through moments of anger, frustration, disappointment, and bitterness. However, since you refuse to sit in the truth of how you feel, regardless of how unpleasant, you are forfeiting the opportunity to turn those negative thoughts into positive transformation.

> *Are you avoiding negative emotions because you fear what they will uncover?*

You won't pray about your issues.

You're a leader, so of course, you fast and pray. But in all of your fasting and praying, you aren't asking God to address the areas **YOU** struggle in. Instead, you bring God the things that you are comfortable addressing. You ask for insight and wisdom for your ministry goals and your vision for the house. You have no problem fasting in faith for the enhancement of the building. You don't mind fasting for healing for Sister Johnson. You will pray until you are blue in the face for God to send Brother Coleman's son home. Sadly, you never ask God to help you with the demons you battle every day. I believe you're leaving you out of your prayer closet because you understand that praying about those issues requires you to admit that the issues are real. It's avoidance as a temporary panacea.

You refuse to admit that your past negatively affects your present.

You constantly say things like, "*What didn't kill me made me stronger!*" Or, "*I'm not looking backward because I'm not going that way!*" While these sayings may have some validity, the truth is that you're still hurting. I get it. You feel like the time you have endured between then and now warrants your freedom. But time doesn't heal all wounds... addressing wounds heals wounds. The influence of your friends, family, and social media followers could make you feel like you should be over that pain by now. It's even worse when others who may have also been involved in the past trauma seem to have moved on. So, instead of admitting how it's still uniquely having

Time doesn't heal all wounds... addressing wounds heals wounds.

a negative impact on you, you pretend that you're over it. However, you still cry yourself to sleep some nights. If you hear certain songs, go to certain places, or see connected people, your heart breaks all over again. Whenever you hear or see anything that reminds you of the pain, you instantly feel the same way you felt when it happened. These are all blaring signs that you're not over it. The mask you are wearing is keeping you from experiencing authentic healing.

The mask you are wearing is keeping you from experiencing authentic healing.

You live a double life.

You preach one thing, but your life reflects something completely different. You will rant on and on for hours in the pulpit about adultery, but you're cheating on your spouse. You'll lay your hands on congregants to help them break free from addiction, but secretly, you still enjoy various narcotics. You tell yourself it's okay because you believe you can quit whenever you want to. You know every vulgar lyric from every secular artist, but when you pull up in the garage at church, you are jamming to the Clark Sisters. You live absent of convictions all week long, but your Saturday nights are *reserved for holiness* because you have to preach Sunday morning. You can be flat-out mean and surly to your family on the way to church, but never miss a Sunday to acknowledge your *amazing spouse and children* over the microphone. You live as if God can't observe your behavior outside of the four walls of your church. However, it doesn't really matter because it's not God you're trying to impress. Your biggest concern is looking holy in front of the people He has called you to lead. This, too, is mask-wearing.

You make every issue a spiritual issue.

Contrary to what you'd like to believe, everything isn't the devil. *Some of it is you.* Is your money under attack, or do you have a gambling problem? Are your relationships really under attack? Or do you just lack the ability to properly value those God has placed in your life? Every concern your family has isn't a distraction from hell to disrupt your sermon prep time. If you take a closer look at every problem you face, you will realize that, at times, you are the common denominator. However, you haven't done that because you wear a mask, even when it's just you. It's much easier to blame everything on the devil and spiritual warfare than to remove the mask and courageously confront what you see.

> *It's easier to blame everything on the devil and spiritual warfare than to remove the mask and confront what you see.*

You don't have boundaries.

No matter the day, you are always frantic, overloaded, exhausted, and/or in a rush. You take on tasks God didn't ordain and responsibilities you don't have the capacity for. You let people in with little to no knowledge of who they are and what they may bring into your life. Every leader you meet instantly becomes sis or bro. Every person who admires you automatically becomes a son, daughter, or mentee. You don't set healthy boundaries. You are available to everyone in every way. You mask it by saying that you are an extrovert and you just love people..., but secretly, you just want to be accepted and/or affirmed anywhere you can get it. You rarely take time to rest, and you think that it's because you have so much to do. The truth is, you are afraid to sit still. If you are too still, you might have to deal with the issues relentlessly haunting you. You know that time for self-care may cause you to uncover the truth behind the pain you've been holding on to for years.

Take a deep breath in...

Release slowly....

Let's continue.

In chapter one, I expressed the sole purpose of this work, so I imagine you have some understanding of the journey ahead. Due to the many times you've led others through their healing process, you know that the first step to healing is admitting something wrong. So yes, if you are going to pursue genuine emotional healing, you must first admit that you wear the mask and take the steps to remove it.

Before we continue, may I offer an apology? For many years, the church and society have fed into the myth that in order to lead in a spiritual capacity, one must be perfect and without flaw. As a result of this spoken and unspoken stipulation placed upon spiritual leaders, many find themselves exerting more energy to maintain their cover rather than doing the work to be free to live without the need to cover. Leaders often feel the tremendous weight of expectation to present themselves as flawless before their congregation. This desire doesn't just include masking serious issues; this also means masking when they are tired, fatigued, or emotionally challenged.

I apologize to you for that.

I'm sorry you were made to feel like you couldn't rest and recuperate because it could be perceived as a lack of dedication. *I'm sorry* you were made to feel that your feelings didn't hold the same weight as your congregants. *I'm sorry* you were forced to hide the sheep bites and pretend as if they didn't deeply hurt. *I'm sorry* you were made to feel like grace and mercy were available for everyone...except you. *I'm sorry* you were made to feel like the anointing took away the reality of your trauma.

Though I cannot reverse what you've experienced, I want to let you know right here and now that you deserve the same grace, mercy, empathy, healing, and, most importantly, restoration that you extend to others. God is willing and able to provide that to you. However, He will require the mask in exchange!

You chose to move into this chapter because you are on the brink of making a conscious decision to prioritize your emotional well-being. You realize that if healing is available, *you want in on it*. However, despite your growing willingness, subconsciously, something is still holding you tightly. The possibility of being well sounds good, but the process can appear frightening. I understand. You're wondering...

How will people respond when
they learn I am unwell?

What will happen when my congregation realizes I'm
not the leader I portrayed myself as?

What will they do when they find out that as I led
them through crisis, addressed their brokenness, and
required them to heal, I, too, was undone?

Will they still see me as their leader?
Will they still follow me?

Will they still respect and honor me?
Will they still believe I carry an authentic anointing, or
will they question its validity and potency?

These questions and many more may be, and have been, plaguing your mind. However, I want to pose to you a different set of questions...

What if ignoring your brokenness leads to your demise?

What will you do if your spouse decides they can no longer live with your mask and desires a divorce?

What if your lack of emotional maturity is causing you to only see half of who God is and who you are in Him?

What if the trauma you won't address emotionally begins to manifest physically and renders you unable to continue leading?

How will you feel when your children become adults, and the only memories they have of you are the torment you lived trying to keep up with two worlds?

Healing may be uncomfortable. However, the stakes are much higher if you refuse to undergo the process. It's time to take the mask off!

Breathe in.

Release.

Let's continue.

WHY YOU WEAR THE MASK

Repression *A thought, feeling, or emotion that is NOT expressed.*

Very often, when one suffers from repression, they deny that thoughts, feelings, or emotions even exist. To repress means to hide, and it is a defense mechanism believed to provide protection. Repression may temporarily keep the issues out of the spotlight, but the impact could destroy your life and the lives of those connected to you. Leader, you believed wearing the mask would protect you from unwanted publicity. However, it is more dangerous than you know. Being unaware of our emotions prevents us from recognizing how they could be affecting and harming ourselves and others. Repression distorts our observations of the moment, memories of the past, and expectations of the future. In fact, repression is the culprit behind addiction, abuse, depression, ulcers, stomach, colon, breast cancer, and a plethora of other physical, emotional, and mental dysfunctions. In addition to being afraid of negative spotlights, there are many reasons why individuals choose to repress their thoughts, feelings, and emotions.

> *Repression may temporarily keep issues out of the spotlight, but the impact may destroy your life.*

As we address five top reasons why most leaders wear masks, I pray that you will find the freedom to move past your fear, remove the mask, and receive the healing your soul has been longing for.

#1 Fear of Judgement

In the last ten to fifteen years, society has developed what is referred to as cancel culture. This is the manner in which we throw away individuals, organizations, or ideals that are deemed unacceptable. Sometimes, we hyper-judge others for the very same things that we just haven't been caught wrestling with. As a result, for many leaders, the fear of being judged has rightfully increased. In order to address this fear, you must first understand that it is normal. As human beings, we are wired to desire to be accepted. We naturally aim to present ourselves in a favorable manner. Many fear that if their weaknesses or shortcomings become visible, they will be rejected from the circles they value most. Despite how many wonderful qualities they may have, leaders believe that one or two flaws, or areas for growth and healing, will overshadow all of the positives they have done. The fear of being judged is rooted in a fear of rejection. Again, considering how the world tends to throw away the wounded, this fear is not irrational. However, God hasn't given us a spirit of fear! Leaders must find a way to break free from the mistakes or inadequacies that have become their prisons. If you continue to hide them to avoid being judged, judgment will be the last thing you have to worry about because the secrets themselves will kill you.

The fear of being judged is rooted in a fear of rejection.

Breathe in.

Release.

Let's continue.

#2 Fear of Truth

Masks are typically used to disguise one's identity from others. However, many leaders also use masks to avoid facing the truth of where they really are. Some leaders avoid the truth because they are too lazy to do the work required to heal. However, for many leaders, that is not the case. They avoid the truth because they don't have the pain tolerance to face it. Here's the thing: **The truth can be more painful than the lie.** At their core, they don't aim to be fraudulent or deceitful in their presentation. Sitting in the reality of their trauma seems far worse than trying to disguise it. Consequently, they would rather deal with what comes with being false than coming to terms with painful truths. Removing the mask means admitting they were abused, mishandled, neglected, and/or treated unfairly. Facing the truth means acknowledging that the molestation, rape, betrayal, divorce, death, and bankruptcy actually happened, regardless of the years they spent convincing themselves otherwise.

> *Some avoid truth because they don't have the pain tolerance to face it.*

Across the nation, leaders have chosen to remain emotionally unhealthy in an attempt to keep themselves safe. I understand and recognize that facing the truth can be scary, but it is necessary. Many clinicians wouldn't dare tell you this, but I will… *sometimes things will get worse before they get better.* Right now, you're sacrificing life and life more abundantly because you don't want to add an additional season of pain to your life. Yes, you may have to revisit some things, but if it means that you will be free for the rest of your life, why not have complete freedom as opposed to partial torment? And one thing about living with internal torment: **torment will rob you of the little bit of peace that you try to muster up.** When you count the cost, you'll realize that though facing the truth may be painful, doing so will position you to have more whole days than broken days.

#3 Avoiding Painful Pasts

There aren't many leaders willingly signing up to go down memory lane to address their painful pasts. As a result, the pain they refuse to address negatively impacts everything connected to them. Though you fight to pretend as if the pain never happened, it has become a part of who you are.

...*The pain you won't address* **impacts how you treat your family.**

...*The pain you ignore* **is the driving factor behind how you treat your teams.**

...*The trauma you avoid* **is the root cause of the dysfunction in your relationships.**

Though it may be unintentional, you are forcing everyone and everything around you to deal with the pain you don't have the courage to face. This, leader, is how certain traumas become cycles. Avoiding your challenges won't stop them from becoming generational struggles. What you avoid will visit your legacies. Someone WILL have to confront this. Do you want to pass this off for your children to grapple? Should your grandchildren inherit dysfunctions that take years to discover the root of, all while blaming themselves for thoughts, feelings, and appetites that didn't originate with them? Please don't perpetuate the transferring of more unaddressed pain. It's a high probability that tears are filling your eyes right now because I've just given language to the fact that what YOU are combatting in this season was inherited. Yes, reliving a painful past is guaranteed pain. However, ignoring it will guarantee that someone you love will have to battle a war they didn't even start.

> *Ignoring pain guarantees that your loved ones will battle a war they didn't start.*

#4 Societal Pressures to be Perfect

We live in a filtered culture. We use filters on social media to make our skin look sparkly and smooth in an attempt to present a picture of perfection. Traditionally, people are more drawn to things that look perfect and unflawed. However, leader, the tide is turning in your favor. In the last three to five years, prominent individuals, organizations, and businesses have begun to popularize flaws. In commercials and ads, we see fewer *perfect models* and more of those who look like *everyday people*. Marketing teams around the nation are realizing that consumers are tired of not seeing themselves in the products advertised to them. It appears that being flawed and communicating flaws is the new thing. As this transparency movement unfolds, more people desire authentic presentations.

"And they overcame him by the blood of the Lamb, and by the word of their testimony, and they loved not their lives unto the death."

REVELATION 12:11

Leader, this is the perfect time to prioritize your healing. The very thing you are trying to hide from may be the very thing that allows others to relate to you. You believe that your flaws will destroy what you are building. However, it may be what attracts those you are called to walk into their own healing. Could the growth that you're believing God for come from those who will respond to your real testimony? Could it be that the people who follow you will never get whole until you expose your fractures? As a leader, you are an example. If there's no hope for you, where is the hope for us? When pastors commit suicide, it's the enemy's way of saying to the world, "*Hey, this 'God-thing' really doesn't work.*" As

Could your image of perfection be the hindrance to their deliverance?

you try to uphold your image of perfection, you could be holding up the deliverance of those who follow you. We have to show that this God thing does work because IT DOES!

#5 Ministry Pressures to be Perfect

As we discussed before, all leaders are under tremendous pressure to be perfect. Sadly, this societal pressure magnifies the pressure leaders feel within the church. Society believes that those who profess to be leaders should be further advanced in their ability to keep their lives in order. While this is, in many ways, an understandable expectation, perfection isn't a realistic demonstration. No one is perfect. No one's life is perfect. We all have seasons that are more harmonious than others. But when it comes to how the world views expectations of spiritual leaders, it's increasingly magnified. They think one is qualified to be a spiritual leader because they have a faith that requires higher standards and have eradicated their humanity's longings.

Since society views spiritual leaders in this manner, it's easy for spiritual leaders to forget the shortcomings of the leaders in the Bible they teach weekly. We forget that David was an adulterer, yet God favored him and declared that David was a man after God's heart. We forget that Noah was a drunk, but God used him in the process of cleansing and repopulating the earth. We forget that Abraham, the forefather of faith, allowed two men to walk off with his wife. We forget that Moses had a problem controlling his temper, but God still used him to free a nation. We allow the expectations of a world that does not know God's mercy to make us forget that God uses flawed people all the time. Leader, you cannot expect to be perfect; you will never see it on this side. However, if you step away from the ministry pressure to appear perfect and come face-to-face with your emotional trauma, you can experience healing and restoration that will allow you to experience more harmony & less harm.

Strength is not found in perfection; it derives from our ability to overcome despite challenges. What you wrestle with doesn't necessarily weaken the anointing. Your fight makes the anointing more potent. Leader, you know well that the oil comes from the crushing. The enemy has lured you into wearing the mask to rob you of seeing the power of God at work, even in your weakness. If God only called the perfect, *there would be no one to call.* God calls and utilizes the postured. The quicker you acknowledge your brokenness, the quicker you can experience God's grace and care.

THE MASK STIFLES YOUR RELATIONSHIP WITH GOD

You see, leader, the mask is just a temporary fix. The mask tells you that you can continue to struggle just as long as no one else knows. The mask makes you feel comfortable in the fact that nobody else can tell what you are going through. You believe that the mask keeps you from *looking like what you've been through*, but it is deeper than that. The mask is a deadly façade. And if you keep depending on it instead of going after the healing you deserve, you will remain broken, unfulfilled, and unsatisfied. Here's why. The mask doesn't just keep you from being open with others. **The mask also keeps you from being open with God.**

In order to heal properly, God has to be able to touch our inner world. Deeply rooted behavioral patterns from our past often hinder our ability to experience true maturity in Christ. This is why many leaders find themselves *doing for* God rather than *being with* God. The enemy desires to keep you so busy doing the business of the church that you never spend the time you need with God to develop emotionally. He knows that if we ever truly start to be with God, then we will really get free. We will discuss this further in the next chapter. However, it is vital that you understand that the mask is keeping you from experiencing the true transformative healing power of God in your own life.

THE MASK CAN RUIN YOUR RELATIONSHIPS WITH OTHERS

When we are in pain, we can unconsciously lash out at others. It may be easier to hide your internal struggles from your congregation. However, those who are closer to you are taking a major hit. Yes, leader, your spouse, children, family, and close staff are sitting in the pain you don't have the courage to deal with. Yes, I know you are using herculean strength and might to hide your pain from the world, but when you get into an environment with those who have a lower risk of leaving you, you unconsciously allow the real you to show. It is your close relationships that take the blunt force of all of your repressed frustrations. You use all of your self-restraint for those that you admire, those you are attempting to gain favor with, or those who can immediately remove things from you, and you leave those who love you and have stood with you to go on the real rollercoaster of your emotional dysfunction. And what's sad is that when you lose close relationships, you tell yourself something is wrong with *them*.

Unfortunately, the people God has sent to be in genuine community with you must separate from you to keep themselves safe and healthy. Leader, you don't have the right to mistreat your circle, and you can't assume how long they'll endure your emotional, verbal, or physical abuse. No matter how much you think your avoidance of help is only damaging you, this book has come to reveal that your lack of emotional health is reaching further than you. Your emotional health is directly impacting the health of your relationships. Though they may never have the courage to say it, many around you have been hurt by your hurt.

THE MASK IS DISTORTING YOUR SIGHT

Because they have worn their mask for so long, many leaders have convinced themselves that there is absolutely nothing wrong with them. They have been pushing their issues under the rug for so long that the mountain of mess has become a part of the landscape of their lives. They have tricked themselves into believing it is just a part of their scenery. What if I told you that because you can't see yourself, *you also can't see the people God has called you to lead?* It's possible that the revelation you've been receiving from God wasn't for the people but intended for you. It's possible that there aren't as many issues on your staff as you believe there are, but your compromised sight is magnifying the minor and minimizing the major. It's possible that you keep seeing problems in others because you aren't seeing the problems within yourself. It's possible that your last sermon series wasn't a big hit with the church because you were preaching to yourself and not them.

"You hypocrite, first take the plank out of your own eye, and then you will see clearly to remove the speck from your brother's eye."

MATTHEW 7:5

After the artist Kanye West's private struggles became public, a number of self-proclaimed psychologists made their debut via social media, and many of them were leaders. It was astonishing to watch so many leaders attempt to diagnose Kanye, point out the many signs that the brother had been unwell for years, and offer a prescriptive course of action that he should take. They pulled apart his albums and song lyrics and pointed out the many blaring notices and cries for help from the artist. I couldn't help but wonder what they would see if they properly analyzed their last ten years on the ministry scene. It is so easy for us to point out the illnesses in others, but we fail to see our own sickness. *How much different would life be if we were to fix the plank in our own eyes first?*

REMOVING THE MASK IS A BIG ASK

Asking you to remove the mask feels like you're being required to remove your safety net. I understand that the invitation this book is extending to you seems like it will do more harm to your life than good. However, it is quite the contrary. **The enemy wants you to remain in the dark so that light can never hit those painful areas of your life.** He wants you to believe that removing the mask will leave you alone, desperate, and embarrassed. However, I want to remind you of the confession of the Apostle Paul in Romans 7:14. Though he had a sinful past, Paul allowed God to turn his life around, and he started churches in which he raised leaders to declare the same gospel he once terrorized others for believing. Despite how apparent it was that the hand of God was upon his life, Paul discloses to us in Romans 7:14 that he desired to do good, but the good he wanted to do, he couldn't do. He found himself struggling internally. This testimony from Paul should encourage you to remove your mask and pursue true healing.

If I can be honest, many of the people you are afraid to show *the real you* have many private battles of their own. You can search the world, and you will never find a leader, no matter how powerful, who has not or is not battling with something internal. Having an internal battle does not necessarily disqualify you as a leader, but not acknowledging it and subsequently seeking help for it could. Could it be that your courage to address it will strengthen you all the more for the assignment God has called you to? It's a big ask, but you have **a big destiny**! With the help of God, I believe you can do this!

IMAGINE YOUR LIFE WITHOUT THE MASK

Make no mistake: I completely understand what this chapter asks you to do. Difficult things are easier said than done. I understand that the fear of judgment, facing the truth, reliving the past, and potentially being ridiculed by society and the church are large pills to swallow. However, I challenge you to move beyond your fear of temporary backlash and finally remove your mask. I cannot promise that everyone will be understanding. I cannot promise that you won't become the topic of conversations at dinner tables, staff meetings, group chats, or even on social media platforms. However, I can promise you that the freedom on the other side is so worth it. I can assure you that you deserve to heal, regardless of what others believe or feel. You deserve to show up in life as you are!

Our emotional health is an area that we must actively fight and conquer. Contrary to popular belief, the enemy is not concerned about your name being on a building or a flyer. The enemy is perfectly fine with you being a pastor, growing your congregation, and even charting new territory. And just in case you were wondering, he is perfectly fine with you preaching your well-crafted messages week in and week out. He won't interrupt your flow just as long as he knows that when you go home for the day, *you are just as depressed as you were when you started your day.* That's why this chapter is probably the most vital chapter of them all. If you can make it through this chapter, the others won't be nearly as difficult. If you reconcile to remove the mask, the journey to true freedom will begin.

> *When you reconcile to remove the mask, the journey to true freedom will begin.*

Can you imagine a life in which you wake up every morning, excited to carry out God's will and assignment for your life? Can you visualize a life in which you are not weighed down by fear of exposure because there's nothing lurking in your closet? Can you imagine a life in which the ghosts of your past aren't haunting you at every turn? Can you see yourself authentically leading people to healthier lifestyles because you did the internal work to resolve your past and are now employing healthy strategies of daily wellness? I wrote this book because I can see you on the other side, and you look amazing! I see you having a beautiful, healthy family and a supportive, authentic village of friends. I see you fulfilling the call on your life with confidence and Godly boldness. I see God using you as an instrument to snatch souls from hell and stop generational curses in their tracks. I see you at your absolute best, and the sooner you decide to remove the mask, you, too, will be able to not just envision yourself on the other side but experience yourself there.

Once you've resolved to remove the mask, take a deep breath, release it, and meet me in Chapter Three, where the deep work begins.

Chapter Three

STAY IN YOUR LANE

You are here! I take it that means you're ready to do the deep work. Do you mind if I celebrate you just for a moment? I don't believe we celebrate ourselves enough for the small steps that are actually quite big. When we hit the financial goal for the church building project, we celebrate. When we finally secure employees for positions that will advance the church's vision, we celebrate. When we reach a certain (consistent) number in membership and attendance, we celebrate. My hope is that after reading this book, you, senior leader, will begin to celebrate the private wins.

The world may not know that you are reading this book and making the conscious decision to lead healthier, but you do, and you should celebrate that decision! Despite how difficult it may have been for you, you pressed through the sting of the previous chapters. You've resolved that you will become the best version of yourself, for yourself, and for those you lead. That alone is an accomplishment worth celebrating! The previous section was designed to be an eye-opener. It was your opportunity to examine your heart and look at where you are as a leader. Section One served as an opportunity to remove the mask and face the issues you've been covering up to save face as the leader everyone knows, honors, and loves.

By now, you've learned that the health of your organization relies heavily upon your emotional well-being. However, as you have taken a look at the symptoms that point to your lack of emotional wholeness, you might be wondering, "*How on earth did I get here?*" In this section, we will address the culprits of your current emotional condition with the hopes that as you pinpoint the root, you will walk away from unhealthy practices and cultural beliefs that keep you unwell.

Before we dig into our first conversation for this section, here's a quick disclaimer. As you read, it's natural to feel uncomfortable as you realize mistakes you've made along your journey as a senior leader. As you explore this section, remind yourself that you can't go back and change the past, but you can make better choices today to improve your future. I'm extremely proud of you.

Deep breath in . . . .

Release slowly . . . .

In again. . . .

Release. . . .

Now, let's begin.

Think back to when you first understood the role of a senior leader in the church. If you grew up in church, it was probably as a child. If you started attending church later in life, it might have been when you were new to the faith. How did you see senior leaders? What did you believe they should be? How did you believe they should operate? Your answers may vary based on your proximity to church leadership, your culture, and the environment of the church.

If you're like most, you probably saw senior leaders as invincible, perfect, and powerful individuals. You probably never expected them to have personal issues, desires, goals, or ambitions. In your mind, you probably thought that they were there to meet every need of every congregant, no matter the time or day. Depending on your age, you probably even believed that they lived at the church and the work of the ministry was the only thing they had to do. Though times and church culture have changed tremendously, many individuals still have similar presumptions of a senior leader. What's more noteworthy is that though leaders literally operate in the role, many begin to view their role in the same way. This unrealistic comprehension of the role of a senior leader, among leaders and congregants, is why many senior leaders are emotionally unwell.

To put it plainly, leader, a large reason why you may struggle to remove the mask and take the time away from ministry to rest, receive counsel, and experience a healthy life is that you don't understand the role. How can you take a break when you feel like your church can't survive without you? How can you admit to your congregation that you need a sabbatical when they see you as their superhero? How can you rest when you see yourself as the center of all the church's operations? This improper perspective of your role as a senior leader makes it difficult for you to do anything other than ensure the church's health above all else. However, as we've discussed several times, when the head hurts, the entire body hurts. In this chapter, we will debunk many of the self-debilitating beliefs you have about your role as a senior leader that are keeping you emotionally unwell and expose the unhealthy components of your relationship with the congregation you lead.

Let's start by exploring the concept of church leadership. The idea, study, and understanding of church leadership is still fairly new, so there's no wonder why so many are confused about what senior leaders are responsible for doing within the ecclesial organizations they lead. Before the twentieth century, conversations about leadership were more directed toward individuals who led in politics, education, and business. Towards the end of the twentieth century, the term' leadership' became increasingly widespread in many churches as a collective term to describe the combined team of local church office-bearers, including the pastors, ministers, elders, deacons, or leaders of other ministries. The church recognized that these positions were important to the health and growth of the church. This revelation led to the surfacing of much discussion and debate on the nature and impact of leadership, understanding that if applied to a church context, it must be looked at from a theological lens. We realized that we couldn't lead how the world leads; instead, we must lead with a Christian lens. In an attempt to define church leadership with Christianity at the center, many attached nonbiblical, unhealthy traditions and expectations backed by incorrect doctrine. This is why we now have tons of senior leaders still unclear on what they should and shouldn't be doing and literally killing themselves in the process of *figuring it out.*

THE ROLE AND RESPONSIBILITY OF A SENIOR MINISTRY LEADER

Traditionally, senior pastors arrive in their positions either by a group or governing board's choosing (voting by way of pastoral search committee or collective congregational vote) or by self-appointment if the senior pastor is the church planter, hence leading the laying of the foundation for the church from its genesis. It is important to remember that despite how a senior leader organizationally came into their role, it is a hope that their calling was truly ordained by God. The senior pastor functions as the head leader within the church's organizational context.

Let's explore what this role entails.

1. Being in consistent communication with God through prayer, study, and devotion through the Word of God.

As a senior pastor, your relationship with God will allow you to have God-inspired vision to cast before the congregation to keep the church moving into its destined future.

2. Preaching and teaching the Word of God.

For most churches, this happens two times weekly during a weekend worship experience and a midweek Bible Study.

3. Provide pastoral counseling for congregants.

Many senior pastors conduct multiple counseling sessions with various congregants each week. At churches with large congregations, this responsibility may be shared with or delegated to leaders the senior pastor selects, trains, and guides.

4. Officiating baptisms, weddings, funerals, and baby dedications for congregants.

Many senior pastors are present and involved in the significant milestones within the life of a congregant and the congregant's family. At churches with large congregations, this responsibility may be shared with or delegated to leaders the senior pastor selects, trains, and guides.

5. Overseeing the business matters of the church.

Many senior pastors simultaneously operate as the

CEO of the church organization and make decisions for the business aspects of the organization according to the church's God-given vision, mission, and bylaws. This responsibility may include overseeing the allocation of the organization's funds, building partnerships with the community and city to further the church's vision and mission, exploring assets for the organization, consulting with legal professionals to protect the operations of the organization, and regular meetings with the organization's board of directors and outside stakeholders.

6. Providing leadership, direction, and vision for leaders, volunteers, and staff of the church.

This looks different depending on the size of the congregation and the church's staffing. At larger churches, senior pastors may frequently meet with teams that oversee larger teams and departments within the church and meet with the body at large on a less frequent but consistent basis. At smaller churches, senior pastors may meet directly with all leaders to give instruction and cast vision.

BEING A SENIOR PASTOR IS A FULL-TIME JOB!

Overall, as it relates to the church, the senior pastor is responsible for ensuring that God's mission and vision for the church are being accomplished. Pastoring is a full-time vocation. It's a job in which the tasks are spiritual and secular. Many of you reading this are probably wondering where the rest of the bullet points for the senior pastor's job are. You're thinking, surely, she left out the part about attending congregants' birthday cookouts. Where's the part about making house calls for congregants who are not feeling well? Aren't we supposed to be at all the Little League softball tournaments? When will she mention the part about visiting the hospital when our members are sick or have babies? What about new house and business blessings? What about stepping in to run choir rehearsals or reset production equipment? This description is missing something!

Well, leader, take a deep breath. Nine times out of ten, many of you reading this book have spent the vast majority of your time as a senior Pastor doing things that are not in God's job description for the role. Decades ago, congregations had great expectations to have a direct and personal relationships with their senior leaders. They desired more than hearing them preach on Sunday; congregants desired to spend time breaking bread with their pastor. Historically, people would invite pastors to their homes to enjoy meals with them. However, this was mostly because people didn't go to restaurants back then, as most, especially African Americans at that time, couldn't afford that. Congregants would contend to have the pastor come to their home for a meal after church and would consider it a great honor to have them at the table with their family. Also, during this time frame, they expected the pastor to attend family events such as graduations, house blessings, baby showers, sporting games, and other life events.

Though times have changed tremendously, many congregants still have these anachronistic expectations of their senior pastors. They may not verbalize it, but in their hearts, that's their desire and expectation. In keeping true to tradition, many senior pastors have done their best to fulfill their congregants' expectations to have a close relationship with them. The sad revelation is that many pastors strive to be there for the personal needs of their congregants at the expense of their own needs being met, their health, their time with their family, and most importantly, rest. It's no wonder why so many senior pastors are emotionally unwell. When you factor in the congregants' personal needs, preparation time for preaching, attending to the church's business affairs, and meetings with staff and team, there isn't much time left for pastors to receive counseling, get rest, and spend time on things they enjoy. It isn't because God has assigned pastors to carry this much responsibility but because many senior pastors have taken on many of these unnecessary burdens, thinking it was a part of the job.

> *Many pastors strive to be there for the personal needs of their congregants at the expense of their own needs.*

In order to debunk this myth and move forward in a healthy relationship with your congregations, it will have to begin with the head. While showing up for every congregant's needs and desires may be noble, it's not God's requirement for the role.

Take a deep breath in . . .

Annnd release . . .

We will work through this together.

Just so that we're clear, let's review a few things you are NOT responsible for as a senior pastor . . .

Being personally and physically involved in every aspect of the congregants' lives.

<u>Two types of leaders will have an issue with this.</u>

...Those who believe their congregants should consult with them about everything for their approval as an authoritarian in the congregants' lives.

...Leaders who feel like God requires them to be there to provide spiritual guidance in every major decision they encounter.

Senior pastors must understand that we don't own congregants. They are actually not "our people." They belong to God. You aren't the head of their lives; you are the servant leader of your congregation as it relates to spiritual teaching and the operation of the business of the church. God doesn't require you to be involved in every decision congregants make for their lives. Senior Pastors are responsible for preaching and teaching the

Word of God and ensuring that congregants gain the spiritual maturity they need to make their own Godly choices through worship encounters and learning environments within the church. The goal is to guide them to God...not for the senior pastor to become their God. Don't worry. We will unpack that a bit more in this chapter.

Being available for every need of the congregants.

In many churches, senior pastors feel responsible for being there for every issue, ailment, and problem that occurs in congregants' lives. The church community knows that if a problem arises in their lives, their senior pastor is just a call away. If Sister Lisa is having backaches again, her family knows to get Pastor on the phone to pray. If Brother Rick has issues paying his rent, he knows how to contact Pastor for benevolence. For congregants, it may sound attractive to have this kind of support from Pastor. However, what kind of condition does this leave a senior pastor in? Tired, worn out, and emotionally unhealthy.

Your commitment to your congregation is to edify. The Word edification is defined as the moral, spiritual, or intellectual instruction or improvement of a person. You are responsible for edifying the body through the Word of God. What was the purpose of that month-long series about faith if your congregants aren't exercising faith in God to meet their needs? What was the purpose of the class on prayer and intercession if congregants still call you for prayer about every small occurrence? When do they get to apply the instruction you spent days in God's Face preparing for them? If congregants were to actually walk out the instruction they received from the sermons they hear, they wouldn't need pastoral counseling. You may not be able to stop them from making the request, but you have a responsibility to redirect them back to the Word. If not, they will continue to rely upon you and not rely upon God. You don't want to consciously or unconsciously set yourself up as an idol to the congregation you serve.

Attending every major and personal event in their congregant's lives.

For years, many senior leaders have found themselves at the hem of every pivotal moment in their congregants' lives. They attend every court date, baby shower, hospital visit, going-away party, basketball game, and graduation. It's no wonder why the families of so many senior leaders feel as though they share their loved ones with the ministry. Contrary to popular belief, the relationship between the pastor and the congregation isn't as personal or direct as congregants would like to make it. Again, being a senior pastor is a vocation, a job. The job is a spiritual responsibility. You're probably thinking, "*But Dr. Khaalida, senior pastors are supposed to relate to the sheep? How can we relate to them if we don't spend time with them?*" I'm not saying that senior pastors shouldn't connect or relate to their members.

However, we must examine how we go about doing this. You don't have to show up in congregants' personal environments to relate to them. You shouldn't want to do this anyway, and they honestly shouldn't desire to have you there! Can we be real for a moment, Pastor? Do you have your own friends and family to enjoy? How are you enjoying the people in your life if you are always attending a function that one of your congregants is hosting? Do you want to know the harsh but freeing truth? Often, they don't want you there because you're you. They don't want you there because of your jokes or because you may have such an infectious personality. They want you there because you are the leader. They want to be able to say, "**PASTOR** was there."

> *Pastor, they don't want you there because of YOU. They want you there because of your ROLE.*

Most people are usually one of two things: *intimidated* by authority or *inspired* by authority. Either they aren't comfortable with leadership, or they want to be around leadership for the power they believe it represents. Those who are attracted to power and authority love being around those who have it. Even if they don't have it, being around it makes them feel empowered. In their mind, their importance is validated by their proximity to you. They don't want to be around you, but more so what you represent. It makes them feel special and important because they have a relationship with the pastor. Guard yourself against the false belief that the people are solely into you. The truth is, many are not. When you do something they disagree with, they will easily defame your name within and outside of the congregation. Your congregants and ministry leaders can make 50 mistakes (some of which could have been detrimental to the ministry), and your "job" is to cover them, correct them, retrain them, and restore them, but if you, as the senior leader, make one error, you will not receive the same. They will leave and look for a "better leader."

When someone can so quickly dismiss you, they never truly cared about you. It was about your role. They want your role in their house, not you. They want your role at Little Keisha's graduation, not you. They want your role at Sister Earlene's repast, not you. And the truth is, they don't even truly know you to deeply care for you. You are ignoring your family's needs, your friends' celebrations, and your endeavors to be around congregants who may only want the presence of your role, not you! And if you think that's not the case, you only need to not show up once and watch how they respond.

The truth can sting, but it's necessary for your freedom, leader! Learn to lead with genuine love and concern from within the boundaries and guardrails of healthy pastoring. Make yourself available for counsel and support, but do it on the days you have allocated for that purpose. Hold those sessions in your office to keep the lines of respect and professionalism clear. Attend some of the fellowships hosted by ministries within the church, and enjoy the beauty of koinonia, but be sober on the relational difference between the congregants you serve and your personal friendships. There should be a distinct difference. Now, are there exceptions to this? Of course! On occasion, you will develop close relationships, usually with those who serve on your executive team. Years of 3-5 days a week building, strategizing, working lunches, and late-night planning dinners will definitely ensure a bond is established. But even in that, don't forget your first and primary assignment in their lives, and that is to be their Pastor! It's your job to establish and maintain healthy boundaries between you and those you serve. It is not the congregants' job; it's YOUR job!

Take a deep breath in...

Now release...

Let's continue...

When you are *too personally* involved, it's easy to take things *too personally.* That's why it broke your heart every time someone left the ministry to go in a different direction. If you were honest, you would admit that it wasn't because of *all you invested* and the *high hopes you had for them to lead in the ministry.* It was because your involvement in their lives made you unconsciously believe they were in relationship with you and not with your particular branch of Zion for the season that God allowed. This is also why you are devastated when congregants do things that offend you. Instead of seeing them as sheep needing guidance, you saw them as friends or family members who owed you some form of personal loyalty. *Again, you took it too personally.* This happens when boundaries between pastors and congregants are blurred or undefined. It's okay to desire to connect with your congregants, but you must ensure that you apply the appropriate boundaries. Failure to do so will continue to negatively impact your emotional well-being and theirs.

Many of you are struggling to accept the truth about your actual role because, for so many years, this is what you were taught to do in order to be a *good pastor.* However, when you stick to the true role and assignment, congregants will feel they have a good, healthy pastor. Just think about it. How much time are you spending in consecration throughout the week if you are at every social gathering your congregants host? What was the purpose of delegating responsibility to other leaders in the ministry if you are still going to take on every need your congregants have? Why does your church even have tribes and small groups if you are still going to strive to be friends with every congregant? Much

> *Most of the personal interaction congregants desire from senior leaders take leaders away from their actual spiritual responsibilities to the church.*

of the personal and direct interaction that congregants desire from senior leaders take the senior leader away from their actual spiritual responsibilities to the church.

Take a deep breath.

If you still struggle to comprehend why you must set healthy boundaries between yourself and congregants, you may be battling in one or more of the following areas.

A Savior Complex *A state of mind in which an individual believes that they are responsible for saving or assisting others.*

Savior Complex symptoms stem from your need to be needed and your belief that you are responsible for meeting the needs of everyone connected to you. It is a strong belief that everything and everyone will falter without you. This is a dangerous mindset to have, and if undealt with, will lead to the detriment of the senior leader. Even though you may not intend to, these actions encourage a misplaced dependence that causes your congregation to see you as their savior rather than Jesus Christ.

What's the point of all the classes and training if you never allow the people to learn and experience God on their own? How can you expect them to build that faith muscle if you run to their rescue every time they have a need? How can you expect them to grow in prayer and communion with God if you're always calling them into your office to pray them through every situation they encounter? In your encounters with congregants, is the emphasis on building a relationship with *you*, or is the emphasis on building their relationship with *God?*

As a senior leader, you must ask yourself the hard questions in order to become emotionally well. I know what you teach them weekly, but upon whom do your **ACTIONS** teach them to rely? I know you encourage them to honor God in your weekly exhortations during worship, but who do your **EXPECTATIONS** direct them to worship and honor?

Most individuals struggling with a savior complex grew up in homes where adult responsibilities were placed upon them too early. They possibly had parents or caregivers who worked long hours and depended on them to care for their younger siblings while they were at work. Or, they had parents or caregivers who had physical, mental, or emotional impairments, and thus, they had to be there for their family in ways children should not be expected to show up. We also see this in some males who grew up in single-mother homes and were often given "man of the house" responsibilities as children. Leader, it may not be your fault that you have a savior complex, but it is your responsibility to heal and realign with your true responsibility. Jesus Christ gave up His life for the church, so you don't have to. The church already

Jesus Christ gave up His life for the church, so you don't have to.

has a savior. God is more than capable of meeting the needs of you, your family, and every member of the congregation you serve. Free yourself today from the burden of attempting to meet every need of the every congregant.

Dependency *The excessive emotional or psychological expectation for a person or an entity to meet a need that is out of alignment with their intended purpose.*

In regards to our conversation, dependency is your excessive emotional reliance on congregants to meet your needs. What needs might that be? Maybe your need to have your ego stroked often? Or, maybe your need to feel needed? Yes, congregants do have unhealthy expectations of leaders. We've discussed and unpacked that. Now, leader, you must inspect the health of your expectations. Remember, everything starts with leadership. Is it possible that you have an unhealthy reliance on your congregants? Is it possible that you keep taking pastoral counseling sessions, even though the elders are trained and available, because you need to feel needed? Is it possible that you have to be the one to make every hospital visit because you don't want to be forgotten? How do you feel when you delegate things to other people, and now, members are giving attention to and developing a relationship with other leaders within your church? You can say

Are you emotionally reliant on congregants to meet your needs?

all day that you don't want the attention, but if you are emotionally unwell, your actions and expectations might be communicating otherwise.

Senior leader, members aren't there to satisfy your emotional needs.

They are not there to satisfy *your anything*.

They **are not** there for you.

<u>They do not owe you anything.</u>

You want members to be faithful to God. If they join, you want them to attend regularly in the hopes that it will assist them to grow in God. You want them to give, not just so the church can have money, but because giving is a part of God's financial stewardship plan for their provision and prosperity. Your hope should be that the power of God will transform members' lives. You should desire that they receive the Word of God through sermons and Bible studies, which will encourage and compel them to add the Word to their daily lives.

Take a deep breath in. . .

And release. . .

Now, let's discuss the next possibility for your inability to set healthy boundaries between yourself and the congregation.

A Way of Escape *A form of temporary distraction from reality or routine.*

This one may be difficult because *we are not supposed to talk about it.* However, we must if you are going to get well. Many leaders use the church to escape from either the demons they're battling or the feeling that their life is unsatisfying outside of ministry. You can be sure that you're using the ministry as a way of escape when you always want to be at the church seven days a week and expect your members to do the same. Do you stay at the church for hours after the benediction because you don't want to go home and deal with your broken marriage? The challenge with that is it keeps you from the time needed to invest in your marriage improving, and now, because you kept the church leaders at the church with you all day, their marriages are falling apart as well. Pastors who do not have healthy home lives always expect something to be happening at the church. They have three services on Sunday, leadership meetings on Monday, Midweek Bible Study on Tuesdays, Soup Kitchen on Wednesdays, Team Development on Thursdays, Movie Night on the Lawn on Fridays, Community Service on Saturdays, and they attend every event.

Pastors with healthy home and personal lives lead very differently. Understand that when I say *healthy*, I don't mean *perfect* — I mean *healthy*. Healthy does not mean without challenges. Healthy means . . .

I've *done the work* to heal from past trauma.
I'm AWARE of my emotions.
I have **proven tools** to navigate my internal world toward positivity.

Healthy pastors with a healthy home and personal life will not demand that members and leaders be at the church every day of the week but will encourage members to build a healthy life OUTSIDE the church. Pastors, you must ask yourself:

- Have I made the church my bride when she is Jesus' bride?
- Have I made the church my social space where I can be entertained and celebrated?
- Am I using the body as an escape so I don't have to address the things happening in my life?

If the answer to any of those is a truthful *yes*, then it's time for you to enter a season of healing.

Traditionalism *The upholding or maintenance of past traditions and practices, especially so as to resist change.*

Much of what we do in the church context has been passed down from previous generations. The actual term for it is embedded theology. Some traditions are beautiful, whereas others are nonbiblical and oppressive, lending them to being detrimental to the health and progression of the church. Many of you reading this book are probably struggling to implement healthy boundaries between your life and your vocation because your predecessors taught you that ministry always comes first. You were taught to always avail yourself to the ministry's needs, no matter the time or day. You watched for years as your church heroes became utterly exhausted, all in the name of ministry. They believed that their relationship with God was the same as the work they did for the ministry. The truth is, who you **ARE** to God and what you **DO** for God are two different things. God designed us as human **BE**ings, not humans **DO**ings!

As a result of this misconception, most pastors have realized that their priorities are out of order. The correct order is God, self, family, local faith community, and whatever your vocation may be. When you go in the correct order, the church doesn't get what's left of you, as many believe. THEY GET THE BEST OF YOU. They are getting a leader who is in tune with God. They are getting a leader who is well-rested, emotionally healthy, physically healthy, socially satisfied, and stress-managed. They are getting a leader who has been loved well from spending consistent quality time with those who care about them. You must combat the thought that the bottom of the list gets the scraps. An appropriately ordered list ensures that everything on the list gets the best. Only when your life is in the appropriate order can you give the church a whole leader. It's a reorienting of priorities.

If you talk to any leader who is 60 or older, they will tell you to reorganize your priorities. Those older pastors can testify about the pain they saw in their children's eyes as they sat and talked about how much they needed their parents and didn't have them because they were at the church too often. Leader, understand that **God is not asking you to sacrifice your family on the altar of ministry.** Release the misguidance that was passed down to you. It will save you from the pain of divorce, the pain of hearing your children confess that when they needed you most, you were never there, and the pain of having to hear that the whole time that you were genuinely trying to do the right thing, you weren't doing the healthy thing. Leader, your life matters, too! Your time matters, too! Your family matters, too!

WHERE DO WE GO FROM HERE?

Until we are honest and establish healthy boundaries between the pulpit and the pew, the church will remain unhealthy. Yes, there are many things we have to address within the pews, but here's the thing. The pew is supposed to be unwell. They are supposed to have a need to heal. That's why they come to what we metaphor as a hospital.

The pulpit, however, should be further along in wellness than the pew! Those trusted to serve from the pulpit should be able to perceive when the pew has unhealthy expectations and not acquiesce to them. However, when a leader is not well, they often can't see the lack of wellness in others. A church where the pew and the pulpit are on the same level of emotional brokenness is a dangerous place for anyone to be.

Realizing that there could be an unhealthy dynamic between you and the congregation can be difficult, but rest assured that there are things you can do to begin to turn the situation around. Yes, there may be disappointment in the culture due to unmet expectations that were never communicated or agreed to. However, as the leader, you must have the courage to reframe dynamics, restructure access, and redefine roles and expectations – despite the kickback you may receive.

Leader, I know that what I'm suggesting is a risk. It's a risk because change is not easy. A lot of people aren't versed in it. Heck, this whole book is a risk, but the question is, are you willing to lose a little now or lose a lot later? Will some people reject a healthier pastor? Will some people reject a healthier community? Possibly. However, have the courage to make the turn for yourself and your congregation's health. Eventually, your courage may cause them to lean in with interest, and they will also end up coming along for the ride. They may not be on board initially, but it doesn't matter when you come on the ride as long as you eventually take the ride.

Even if you first have to walk alone, my prayer is that you will experience the beauty and fullness of walking with God. Some may have to part, but more will become a part! The health of your organization relies on your well-being. The change may not initially *feel good*, but it will definitely develop to *be for the good* of that which God has entrusted you to establish, build, and lead.

Chapter Four

STILL SHEEP

Before we begin, *take a deep breath*. Perhaps deeper than you've taken all day. *Take another deep breath in... now out*. Throughout this book, there have been intentionally placed reminders to breathe. Breathing offers our minds and hearts the opportunity to accept, process, recenter, and become present within the weight of transformative truth. Our breath is the most simplistic, constant reminder of our dependency on God. There is much we can accomplish and do for ourselves. We can purchase luxuries to make our lives more comfortable. We can indulge in activities and relationships to make our lives enjoyable. However, every time we take a breath, we are reminded that without the very breath of God, none of it would be possible. And that, leader, is the intent of this entire chapter: **to gently push you back into the place of awe, wonder, and total dependency on God as His child.**

Think it not strange that you are in need of this reminder. Even King David, with all his achievements, victories, riches, property, etc., had to welcome the reminder of his dependency on God. In Psalm 23, verse one, King David states, "*The Lord is my shepherd.*" When you think of the role of a shepherd, it wasn't a prestigious job. It was thought insignificant, so much so that it was typically given to the youngest in a family. However, of the many things David knows God to be, of the many things David could say about the Lord during his reign, he calls him his Shepherd.

David fully understood the role of the shepherd. He knew that a shepherd had a personal relationship with the sheep. The shepherd guides the sheep daily and ensures they are covered and protected. The shepherd knows each sheep intimately, so he is aware if a sheep is missing. The shepherd puts oil on the heads of sheep to ensure they don't bash their heads, trying to rid themselves of gnats and other flying pests. The shepherd knows when the water may be too high and might weigh sheep down. But there is a greater Shepherd that was the originator of shepherding. This Shepherd is mighty and powerful, our Lord, our Savior, our King. Being trusted by the Great Shepherd to serve HIS flock as an undershepherd should never leave us thinking that the Great Shepherd has retired. So if, in fact, HE is The Great Shepherd, then WE, LEADERS (all of us, regardless of title, office, position, membership count, social media following, financial assets, and dividends), must be HIS sheep. A great theologian, bishop, and true church statesman said it this way many years ago...

"Herein lies the schizophrenic dynamic of the clergy position. We are called upon by God to wear two hats. We are both shepherd and sheep. We cannot escape our sheep-ness. For even when we function in the role and the anointing of being a shepherd, there's something about my sheep-ness that is hard to contain. My sheep-ness is so unpredictable that I can't manage it myself. I'm a shepherd of sheep, but yet I'm a sheep that needs a shepherd."

BISHOP ULMAR

My question to you, Pastor, is, though you have responsibilities to undershepherd others, are you still allowing yourself to be shepherded daily? Are you still allowing yourself to be covered & protected? Are you still allowing oil to be put on your head to ensure you don't bash your head trying to rid yourself of distracting gnats and destructive pests? Are you still allowing your shepherd to tell you when you've gotten into a situation that may be too high for you or has the potential to weigh you down?

Do you realize that **YOUR** *shepherd knows when you're missing?*

Pastor, are you allowing yourself to be known by God intimately, or has your working **FOR** Him caused you to forfeit intimacy **WITH** Him? Beyond what you say and present to the pews...*Is the Lord really YOUR*

Shepherd? Or, is it that after all of your preaching, prophesying, leading, evangelizing, pastoring, building, and edifying, you are yet far from God? For many of you, the quote from Bishop Ulmar brought about a sense of relief, a reminder that as you carry the weight of being the senior pastor, you are not carrying it alone. Just as you shepherd the people, you, too, have a shepherd to lean to and run to in times of need. What is critical for clergy leadership to remember and daily embrace is that you are NOT your own Shepherd! Furthermore, when it comes to the members of the local body you serve, You are not THE Shepherd; you are an **UNDERshepherd.** For in John 10:14-15, Jesus says...

"*I am the good shepherd; I know my own sheep, and they know me, just as my Father knows me and I know the Father. So I sacrifice my life for the sheep.*"

JOHN 10:14-15

It should relieve us of some pressure to know that there is a Supreme Shepherd, and when we are done in moments being used by Him to minister to HIS sheep, we, too, are shepherded by Him. We get to relinquish responsibility in moments of vulnerability, and we too can come to the Father for comfort, consolation, and salve. It is all too easy for congregants, after witnessing the transforming impact of the Gospel, to see the senior leader as some sort of superhuman. But the truth is, you aren't superhuman. Are you? *You hurt. You experience disappointment. You go through seasons of trial and tribulation.* And, regardless of what the congregation may believe, *you don't have all the answers.* So, when did you allow the needs of the people to make you lay down your need for God? When did you forget that much like those you've been entrusted to lead, you, too, are a sheep in need of a shepherd?

HOW DID WE GET HERE?

Leader, it is dangerous to lead without acknowledging that you are still sheep. How can you feed congregants afresh if you haven't eaten afresh? How can you cast vision if you haven't sat before God to receive vision? Furthermore, how can you comfort and aid His sheep as they navigate life if you haven't availed yourself to receive comfort and aid for your life path? For many of you, the congregation's growth is stagnant because your spiritual growth has been stagnant. You are studying to write sermons for the people, but you don't do devotions so God can speak to you. Congregants are ready for more, but you can't provide it. True spiritual revelation comes by way of relationship, not academics. So, before you have another team meeting to discuss the issues you perceive with the church God has entrusted you to lead, can I challenge you to examine the state of your spiritual health? How is your personal walk with Christ? Are you being shepherded? Let's explore the possible culprits that led you to forget that you are still sheep.

1. The people made you their God, and you didn't correct them.

Many people who enter our churches on Sunday mornings have been let down and disillusioned by what's occurring in the world. As a result, they desperately need something to believe in. Very often, it is hard to place their hope solely in an invisible God. Therefore, they place this hope in the senior leader, who they can physically see. Sometimes this is done consciously, but often it's done unconsciously. When congregants see their leader operate in the supernatural, prophecy, or be used by God as a conduit to administrate miracles, signs, and wonders, they are in awe of the anointing. When they hear their pastor deliver a powerful message that brings them to tears, many develop a reverence, not just for God, who empowered the leader, but also for the leader themselves.

As a senior pastor, you may read this and think, "*I can't help how people perceive me.*" While this may be partly true, you, leader, have a responsibility to ensure that you always point people back to God. When they come up to you after you've finished preaching and say, "*Pastor, thank you for freeing my mind today,*" you can respond by saying, "*I'm grateful that Jesus brought liberty to you today.*" Not facilitating every meeting because your ministerial team can handle some of the congregant care and every congregant crisis not requiring your immediate attention and presence (as discussed in the previous chapter) can lessen their view of you as their God. And it's okay for church events to take place where you aren't the facilitator. It is vital that you take a step back to understand the role you may be playing in people's dependency on you.

2. Your church's culture is leader-focused rather than God-focused.

Though we don't want to admit it, in many churches, the culture is focused too heavily on the leader rather than God. Many have succumbed to a theology of leadership based on an individual rather than on claiming the power of God-led stewardship within a robust, healthy community. It is all too easy for a theology of leadership to set up a leader who has charisma, intellect, and even physical attractiveness, as opposed to a leader who is spiritually mature, emotionally healthy, intelligent, and sensitive to the moving and workings of the Spirit of God, and is fully in submission to God first in all things. **A church solely centered around the personality, fame, and/or personal preferences of a leader rather than God is unhealthy and will breed an unhealthy community of idolatry.** This often ensures that what the leader says and displays won't be properly weighed. If the people can quote your "sayings" more than they can quote scripture, leader, we have a problem.

3. Your success measurement tool is flawed.

According to our culture, the prime examples of successful leadership are leaders who have amassed tremendous influence and financial wealth. This can be dangerous because it becomes a question of who the leader knows and what the leader possesses, as opposed to who the leader is. The people "*ooh and ahh*" at every major accomplishment or new influential connection you make, and you go through great (sometimes unintegral) measures to ensure you keep their awe. As a result, they fail to recognize that God, not your accolades, made you the leader. And you, Leader, out of a desire to maintain what they believe, forget that you are still a sheep yourself, and but for the grace of God, nothing you have amassed would be obtainable or maintainable! Every success you or your ministry experiences is due to God. All Glory belongs to God. Leaders who acknowledge that they are still sheep don't measure success by what the world can see but rather by what God knows.

Every success you or your ministry experiences is due to God. All Glory belongs to God.

4. You have exalted yourself.

Leader, it is dangerous to see yourself more highly than you ought. Not only does this impact your view and actions, it directly impacts those you lead. When you exalt yourself, you create an environment wherein those you lead place you on a level that is too high for you to achieve. And when you fail or make a mistake, because you will, those who follow your lead become distraught. Why? Because they held you in a space of perfection reserved for God. As a senior pastor, you must ensure that the congregation God has entrusted you to manage does not forget relationship of community and recognizes that all success, gifts, and graces belong not to the leader but are from God.

5. The pressures of being a "perfect" leader

It is not beyond me that the pressure and expectations people have of leaders can cause you to feel like you are no longer sheep. Sometimes, leader, you do everything you can, and people are still ungrateful. You live upright and maintain healthy boundaries, but the people still question, gossip, and speculate about you and your life. This book is just for you, so we can be honest here. At times, it can feel like what you do is never enough. No matter what decisions you make, someone will be unhappy about it. You wonder why those that you lead expect to receive grace, yet extending it to you seems to not be an option. This is why it is mandatory that you never forget you, too, are sheep, and allow The Shepherd to heal you of sheep bites from those you've been entrusted to undershepherd, as well as remind you that His grace is, in fact, available for you.

Furthermore, God put you in this seat of authority, so be free from congregants' unreasonable expectations of perfection. There will always be people who feel like they can do the job better, but many of them are assessing a seat they have never sat in and have a limited view of. They will never understand the weight that comes with being a Senior Leader if they have never been one. They can't comprehend the early mornings, long nights, 15-page weekly sermons, pastoral counseling sessions, funerals, and expense management, just to name a few. But what if I told you they're not supposed to? They may not know, but God knows. And not only does God know, but God cares. That's why, despite how they may see you, you can NEVER lay aside your reliance on God. You need 'Him' to manage 'them.'

6. Your deficiencies collided with their expectations.

There is an insidious cycle that creates an impenetrable loop of leaders being held on pedestals that seem to go higher and higher the more successful the appearance of the particular church. Because God's holy perfection and inherent goodness often feel abstract and intangible, people look to you, leader, for glimpses of the divine in action. However, the last thing some leaders need is a steady diet of being told how holy, perfect, and righteous they are. An inherent performance-based standard within a leader who struggles with ego issues, narcissism, a savior complex, or any other character/ personality flaws becomes fueled by such attention and adoration that was only intended to be attributed to God. It, in turn, inflates that leader's self-worth to the point where they either go into denial and self-delusion over their shortcomings and moral failures or compartmentalize them into a hidden, secret part of themselves that no one must ever discover. Sadly, when their transgression is eventually discovered or exposed, or when they confess because the weight of their burden has compressed their emotional spine to the point of threatening their life and sanity, these leaders experience the congregation's contempt for violating their illusion of perfection. Leader, if the people's expectations are causing you to hide your issues, and your issues are making you hide from God, how can The Shepherd ever make you whole? You aren't perfect. You never will be. It's imperative to ensure that both you and your congregants know that.

7. The leaders you look up to don't consider themselves sheep.

Many of those who came before us maintained an anything-but-sheep reputation. We saw *their elevation.* We saw *them being highly regarded.* We saw *them being fawned after.* We saw *them being served*, yet rarely serving. We never witnessed them being sheep. As a result, we have a generation of leaders who served to get OUT of serving. And, now that they have assumed the position of senior leadership, the idea of being anything close to *sheep* is offensive. So no, they won't meet with most of *their* congregants because Bishop So and So rarely met with the members who requested it unless they were "core tithers." And no, they won't admit to faults or flaws because growing up, Prophetess Perfection never even had a hair out of place. The idea of taking even one Sunday off to rest is beyond their imagination because the great Reverend Doctor Whoever preached every Sunday until his dying day. While the previous generation may have never displayed their humanity, they were most definitely human. They had human needs, feelings, and emotions. They were not gods or superhumans. They were men and women. They were sheep. *And so are you.*

Take a deep breath in. . .

And release. . .

I hope reading about these possible culprits opened your heart to explore where and when you fell off track in your relationship with God. Rest assured that all hope is not lost. Despite what it feels like, you can make the necessary shifts in your leadership and personal relationship with God to remember that you will never elevate out of being one of God's sheep. *Take another deep breath.* Let's continue our discussion with a few necessary reminders that are fundamental to your role as an undershepherd.

All Power Comes From God

Leader, if you desire to be healthy and undershepherd a healthy congregation, you must be very clear on this: You only have power through your relationship with Christ to fulfill the mission of the church. The Apostle Paul, though he was a great leader and had the honor of doing great things within the body of Christ, was clear that his credentials were not found in "signs and wonders and mighty works" (2 Corinthians 12:12) or in "lofty words or wisdom" (1 Corinthians 2:1), but solely "with a demonstration of the spirit and of power, so that... faith might rest not on human wisdom but on the power of God" (I Corinthians 2:4). Senior leader, when we forget these fundamental truths, *we invite congregants to develop an unhealthy reliance on our role.* When we forget these truths, *we open the door to unhealthy expectations from our congregations.* When we forget these truths, *we allow people to depend on us more than they depend on God.* When we forget these truths, *we forget that we are still sheep in need of the guidance, wisdom, and care of The Good Shepherd.* Paul's understanding of his role in the church is vital for us as undershepherds. It keeps us sober and keeps us from the temptation to become prideful. It ensures that everyone's focus and reliance remains on Christ alone.

You Can't Work for God Without God

Charles Spurgeon warned leaders against a condition that he calls **MINISTERIALISM.** It means that if we study the Bible more as ministers than as Christians, more to find the matter for the instruction of people than the nourishment of our own souls, then we neglect to place ourselves at the feet of Jesus, our divine teacher. In other words, leader, our personal, private communion with God should never be cut off because we begin to work for God!

Our relationship with The Father yields many great rewards. In our **worship** of the Father, we are strengthened with wisdom and endurance and reminded of where to place our faith. Through **daily prayer,** we are able to go before our Father and both empty ourselves as well as be poured into. Through **consistent devotion,** we are reminded that His compassions fail not. But not only that, God meets our human needs, for we do not serve a God who is not aware or concerned about our needs. The relationship we have with God is one of great intimacy.

Senior Leader, you may be reading and, at this point, believe your intelligence is being insulted. Of course, you already know about the power of being in relationship with God. After all, Sunday after Sunday, you stand within the pulpit and give beautiful words that exclaim the power of being in fellowship with the God of our salvation. Every week, you lead Bible Study, teaching congregants more about God in hopes that they may draw closer to Him. You push the praise and worship team into taking people deeper into worship. You encourage people to give unto the Lord and trust Him to provide for their needs. You, more than anyone, know the power of true relationship with God. However, somewhere in the midst of pouring, preaching, and pastoring, many leaders forget to not only come to God on behalf of the people but also to seek Him on behalf of themselves.

As we do the dance between being undershepherds and sheep, we must appreciate the importance of not only being gifted and anointed but diligently studying the scriptures under the guidance of the Holy Spirit so that we will continue to hold onto the horns of the altar. You CANNOT lead God's church without God. There is a deeply personal transformational experience that must occur and continue to occur in your personal discipleship in Christ. Without the real transformation that is accomplished in this way, ecclesiastical leadership is in, Gregory of Nazianzus says, "*the gravest of dangers*" *and* "*of all things most to be feared.*" It is positively dangerous and a crass exercise of human power to seek to spiritually guide others when one is not being spiritually guided by God. Christopher Beeley, in his work Theology and Pastoral Leadership, notes, "*To think that we can, even partially, save the world ourselves is dishonest, deeply selfish, and often catastrophic for the lives, families, and communities of leaders who attempt to do so. Even if the attempt is unconscious.*"

Admit Your Faults and Shortcomings

If Jesus desired humility and commended those who acknowledged their shortcomings, then leaders, we must do the same. We must be mindful not to adopt Pharisaic thinking and behavior. This is seen in the parable found in the Gospel according to Luke. Jesus tells the story of two men who were in church to pray before God. One man, a Pharisee (leader), loudly declared: "*God, I thank you that I am not like other people—robbers, evildoers, adulterers-or even like this tax collector. I fast twice a week and give a tenth of all I get*" (Luke 18:11-12). However, the other man, a tax collector, kept his head down and didn't even feel worthy to come to the altar. His prayer was strikingly different. He prayed, "*God, have mercy on me, a sinner*" (Luke 8:13). Jesus responds, "*I tell you that this man, rather than the other, went home justified before God. For all those who exalt themselves will be humbled, and those who humble themselves will be exalted.*"

A leader admitting their faults, shortcomings, sins, and proclivities, hence their *sheep-ness*, is a leader who is humbling themselves before God. You, leader, deserve the same mercy, grace, and healing love you have told so many are available for them. God is standing with open arms, willing to give this same compassion to you. I want to remind you today that you are a child of God! Choose to no longer be dishonest with yourself or God. Let God usher you out of caves of silence that the enemy would love to keep you locked in. Admitting a dark feeling, emotion, or action is equivalent to turning the light on. When light comes in, darkness has to flee. It is at that moment that light can shine from the pulpit you stand in Sunday to Sunday, not because of a perfect vessel, but because of perfect Grace.

Take Cover!

Every pastor needs a pastor! We could end the chapter there, but because I know that some may struggle with that last statement, let's unpack it. Because what's the real issue, leader? Are you averse to accountability? Are you so controlling that you don't want anyone to weigh in on your decisions? Do you fear the exposure that may come with vulnerability? Or, have you submitted to a covering in a previous season and were mistreated, betrayed, or dropped? If you are a pastor without a pastor, I challenge you to explore your reason why. Welcome God to change how you view having a covering. It's okay to need support as you support others. It doesn't make you weak; **it makes you stronger**. Having a covering doesn't take away from you. Rather, **it adds to you.** It can lengthen your chords, add quality to your leadership, and expand your reach. Most things last a little longer when, instead of being laid bare, instead of being left exposed, it's COVERED! But not just any covering. You don't need a placeholder, someone to just verbally claim as your covering, or someone to just visually place on a graphic for the optics. You also don't need a covering that is spiritually deaf or blind. You need a covering that can see God, that knows that God sees them, and they can see you... all of you.

> *Most things last longer when they are COVERED!*

As we close this chapter, I challenge you to get your "*baaaaaaaaah*" back. You have laid aside your sheep-ness for far too long. I understand that you were trained by leaders who didn't acknowledge their sheep-ness. I also understand that the pressure of the people can make you forget that you, too, are sheep. However, you cannot afford to continue to lead, pour, or minister without remembering that you are still sheep. Humble yourself enough to recognize that you never stopped needing to be shepherded. I know you're an Apostle, but you're still one of God's children. I know you're a Prophet, but you're still one of God's children. I know you're a Pastor, but you're still one of God's children. I know you're an Evangelist, but you're still one of God's children.

"At that time the disciples came to Jesus and asked, "Who is greatest in the kingdom of heaven?" He called a little child and set him before them, and said, "I assure you and most solemnly say to you, unless you repent [that is, change your inner self—your old way of thinking, live changed lives] and become like children [trusting, humble, and forgiving], you will never enter the kingdom of heaven. Therefore, whoever humbles himself like this child is greatest in the kingdom of heaven."

MATTHEW 18:1-3

When was the last time you allowed yourself to crawl into the Father's lap? The consolation, strength, guidance, and healing you need for the next leg of your journey is awaiting you in your Father's loving arms. But first, you must resolve within yourself that despite your calling, the anointing, and the appointing...

You. Are. Still. Sheep.

Chapter Five

YOU ARE THE MAN!

The Transformative Power of the Prophetic Scapel

"Then Nathan said to David, 'You are the man! Thus says the Lord God of Israel: 'I anointed you king over Israel, and I delivered you from the hand of Saul...' 'Why, then, have you despised the word of the Lord and done this horrible deed?' "

2 SAMUEL 12:7,9A

God appoints leaders to organize, cast vision, teach, encourage, guide, and be examples for God's people. There are numerous biblical accounts of leaders who have done just that. Abraham, Moses, Joshua, Gideon, Samuel, and many others obeyed God and led with strength, courage, and integrity. However, because this particular leader's experiences are a mirror for leaders to see themselves, we're going to exegete some aspects of King David's leadership. The account of King David and the Prophet Nathan in 2 Samuel serves as an excellent conclusion to the purpose of this section. So, take a deep breath in and release slowly. As you read through this section, keep in mind that the goal is to support you in seeing the importance of your emotional health. The purpose of this chapter is not only to nudge you towards internal wellness but to ensure that you maintain it as you organize, cast vision, encourage, guide, and serve as an example for God's people.

We are introduced to David in 1 Samuel 16 as the youngest son of Jesse the Bethlehemite. The prophet Samuel is ordered by God to find and anoint the next king of Israel after God rejects Saul. As the story goes, David was not the son that anyone thought Samuel would be looking for, however, after each of his older brothers was presented, none of them were God's chosen. Almost being forgotten, Jesse remembers that he has one more son tending the sheep. Once David was presented, the Lord said to Samuel, "*Rise and anoint him; for this is the one*"(1 Sm 16:12b). The Bible records that once anointed, the spirit of the Lord was upon David from that day forward. In 1 Samuel, we see David's posture of humility and his heart of servanthood while submitting to Saul. He was being prepared for his soon-coming reign.

In 2 Samuel, we are immersed in the recording of David's forty-year reign from 1010-970 B.C. as the leader of all of Israel. 2 Samuel takes us on a journey of excitement as David is crowned king over Judah and all of Israel (5:1-5), joy from him bringing the Ark of the

Covenant back to the tabernacle (6:1-23), and pride as his leadership is seen strongly in his armies' victory over their enemies, completing the conquest of the promise land begun by Joshua (8-10). Unfortunately, despite David's strong beginnings, his dark moments are also highlighted, and 2 Samuel provides us with a clear view of what can happen when a leader's integrity falters due to unaddressed emotional health challenges. King David's sense of entitlement, greed, lust, and calculated murder of one of his own faithful soldiers is revealed, and many innocent people are directly impacted by his actions.

King David, overcome by his lust, had the wife of one of his soldiers, Uriah, brought to him so he could sleep with her (2 Sm 11:3-4). As a result, she became pregnant (11:5), which compelled David to continue committing acts of sin to cover up his original sin. David allowed Uriah to come home from war in hopes that Uriah would sleep with his wife and assume paternity of the child. However, Uriah demonstrated more integrity than King David in refusing to abandon his military assignment and enjoy himself while his brothers were at war (11:6-13). As a result, David arranged for Uriah to be killed in battle (11:14-24).

I don't know about you, but I am grateful that the repercussions of David's actions were included in our canon, as it is imperative that we, as leaders, see a full picture of what can happen to those who misuse or abuse God's delegated power. This story serves as a warning that regardless of how powerful one is, God disciplines even those we may think are untouchable. There will never be a king in our land that is above the King of Kings; that is above chastening from God.

After the death of Uriah, David made Bathsheba his wife and had seemingly gotten away with his sin, but the Lord knew about it and sent the prophet Nathan to rebuke David. Nathan went to David and wisely told the king a fable about a rich man and a poor man: the rich man was visited by a traveler, so he took the poor man's only possession, a little ewe lamb that he loved as a pet, to feed his guest—rather than taking a lamb from his extensive flocks. David was enraged at the story and declared that the rich man had no pity and deserved to die. Unfortunately, David was so blind to his previous actions that he could not see himself in the parable. David did not make the connection that he was the rich man and Uriah was the poor man. So great was his disconnect that he became furious and ordered death for any man who would do what the rich man did (12:5). Additionally, David ordered the rich man to repay what he stole and chastised him for his lack of pity (12:6). It is fascinating to witness how clearly one can see outside of themselves, but not inside themselves. God knew that David was so comfortable

There will never be a king in our land that is above chastening from God.

in his authority that he was unaware of his misuse and abuse of power. It would take a prophetic voice to come in and speak truth to power.

The prophet Nathan then points to David and says, "*You are the man!*" (2 Samuel 12:7). Nathan reveals that David's sin was like that of the rich man because David took away Uriah's wife. Nathan then prophesies to David, in God's own words:

"*I anointed you king over Israel, and I delivered you out of the hand of Saul. And I gave you your master's house and your master's wives into your arms and gave you the house of Israel and of Judah. And if this were too little, I would add to you as much more. Why have you despised the word of the LORD, to do what is evil in his sight? You have struck down Uriah the Hittite with the sword and have taken his wife to be your wife and have killed him with the sword of the Ammonites. Now therefore the sword shall never depart from your house, because you have despised me and have taken the wife of Uriah the Hittite to be your wife.*"

2 SAMUEL 12:7–10

David confesses to Nathan that he has sinned against the Lord, and Nathan comforts him, saying that the Lord has forgiven his sin and that David's life will not be required of him. At this powerful, introspective juncture, David, under the inspiration of the Holy Spirit, pens the repentant words within Psalm 51. What a powerful moment in our biblical canon that shows the transformational beauty that can come from prophetic intervention.

King David stands as an example of leaders all over the country who have neglected to confront their inward battles and, as a result, have fallen into traps of self-destruction and harming those they lead. King David's lack of self-awareness regarding the state of his emotional health in that season made it difficult for him to discharge his assigned duties honorably. First, David should have never been home to observe Bathsheba, as he should have been at war, fighting with his men. Second, the thought and effort used to cover up his sin took David's focus away from his kingly duties and put the other soldiers, and frankly, all of Israel, in harm's way. Third, David's actions as a leader "*gave the enemies of the Lord great opportunity to despise and blaspheme God*" (12:14). When we are not physically well, we have no reservations in acknowledging our deficit and seeking care to heal it. However, when we are not emotionally well, we struggle to even view our condition, and then if a glimpse comes to our consciousness, we rush to cover it from ourselves and others. This move of denial at all costs can bring a leader to great panic, which causes them to commit acts of desperation they

When we are not emotionally well, we struggle to view our condition. If a glimpse comes to our consciousness, we rush to cover it.

would have never thought they were capable of. Leader, all of the efforts made to not admit the flaws that are a part of what makes up the fullness of our humanity can cause destruction for your family, followers, and the assignments entrusted to you. You must begin to see and embrace the truth of where you are and what you may be internally struggling with. As clergy, if we fail to do so, we will continue to have leaders such as David and the consequences that follow. How can a leader be strong, courageous, bold, and inviting while also being a betrayer, liar, adulterer, and murderer? Simply by not acknowledging their emotional challenges and seeking help to work through them.

LEADER, YOU NEED A PROPHETIC EXCHANGE

As we are currently immersed in times that seem to encourage leaders to seek self-advancement above others and prosperity at all costs, prophetic voices are much needed. A prophetic voice carries within itself a sustainable, transformative element. Prophetic voices are charged with speaking truth to power. They have a unique ability to compel those in positions of power to see what could be hidden from their view and offer them support in having the courage to make a change for the better. The thought of examining our emotions, confronting past hurts, and connecting our internal feelings to our external choices can be a daunting task. A prophetic voice can masterfully utilize a spiritual scalpel to cut and uncover with precision and great care. They do this not to harm but to help. Prophetic preaching, teaching, and counsel present truth without fear and open the gates for revelation, introspection, and transformation.

The hurdle of confronting emotional challenges is admitting that the challenge exists. Simply, you cannot fix what you refuse to face. Leader, prophetic encounters can assist you in realizing that in a certain season, "*You are the man/woman.*" A prophetic message can be the alarm, clarion call, and clean mirror to bring forth a truth that otherwise would simply not come before you. Did God chastise David? Yes. Did David have consequences for his actions? Yes. But once he received a prophetic message, David humbled himself. In response to the message brought to him by the Prophet, David repented. His fellowship and peace with God were restored, and he was able to continue to lead. However, if God had not sent a prophetic word to awaken him to himself, his life and works could have ended in 2 Samuel 11. But by the grace of God, the prophetic word was given and received, which ushered David to arrive at Psalm 51.

You cannot fix what you refuse to face.

Jesus' ministry was nothing short of prophetic. He was, in fact, the walking embodiment of the prophetic. Although his message was one of love, hope, and salvation, it was also one of discipline, accountability, and kingdom responsibility. As does the prophetic, Jesus attracted hostility in that his presence was often viewed as divisive and provoking due to its root messages being counter-cultural. Jesus' Kingdom message challenged religious idolatry, and his presence aroused the wicked tormenting spirits within the souls of men.

Now, I would be remiss if I didn't give language to the reality that, to this very day, many people are perplexed, concerned, and even cautious of prophetic encounters, whether in public spa, sacred space, or private space. This is understandable because of the unfortunate occurrences that many of you reading this book have either personally experienced or have cringely observed of prophetic moments being grossly mishandled or moments that were nothing but carnal, clownish, self-aggrandizing antics posing as something prophetic and sacred. I apologize for every time you have had to wrestle with the sincerity of a prophetic occurrence or utterance. I pray that you would not give up on the holy, sacred, and beautiful power that can be experienced when you encounter an emotionally healthy prophet who is fully submitted to the Lordship of Jesus Christ. Their presence and utterances aren't a mixture of God and their pain but are a crystal clear flow of God's thoughts to you without man's fingerprints. There are many true Nathan's in the earth today.

Leader, before you can stand to speak truth to power, you must be on the hearing end of some truths. Despite the uncomfortable feelings the prophetic voice may ignite, the hope is that it will inevitably provoke a transformation from prideful positioning to humble servitude. Leader, even if you are prophetic, you still need to be humble enough to receive from God concerning your own life through the power of the prophetic.

DAVID VS. NATHAN

Despite the necessity of prophetic voices, many leaders remain resistant and reluctant to allow these voices in their spaces. Yes, I know you are the leader, and God has given you vision for the ministry you lead. However, leader, allow me to remind you that you don't lead out of what you know. You lead out of who you are. Sometimes, who you are isn't healthy enough to lead in a manner God deems acceptable. In seasons where you are blinded by your emotional turmoil, past unprocessed trauma, or current secret transgressions, you need a prophetic voice to reveal to you that "You are the man." In today's church climate, the relationship between David's and Nathan's is extremely challenged because neither understands the weight of the other. In hopes that the value of this most vital relationship can be seen and grace offered from one seat to another, this section will address both David's and Nathan's. In order for the head (leader) to stop hurting, both of these offices must make some adjustments.

Dear Nathan (Prophet)

Nathan, whose name means (God has given) was a prophet of God, a fearless but careful confronter, and a trusted advisor to David. Like some biblical prophets, Nathan's personal story, birth, family, and death are not always available to us. What matters is not who he is but what he says and to whom. He was one of God's many spokesmen used to speak and counsel those in positions of power despite the difficult messages they carried. We need more Nathan's to, under the leading of the Holy Spirit, speak truth to power and ensure that leaders can become or maintain emotional wholeness.

For every person reading this book, and you are clear that God has called you to the office of the Prophet, you need to be mindful and wise in what you say and honorable toward whom God trusts you to say it. Most prophets are called to give words from God to those who are in positions of leadership. As a result, it is imperative to live in a way where nothing will compromise your ability to be received by a leader or cause you to feel a need to mute what that leader needs to hear. Not only is the leader's future on the line, but the futures of those connected to the leader are hanging in the balance as well.

God is in no way naive to the challenges that come with carrying out your prophetic assignments. God was clear with the Prophet Ezekiel when He said...

"Son of man, I am sending you to the Israelites, to a rebellious nation that has rebelled against me; they and their ancestors have been in revolt against me to this very day. The people to whom I am sending you are obstinate and stubborn. Say to them, 'This is what the Sovereign Lord says.' And whether they listen or fail to listen—for they are a rebellious people—they will know that a prophet has been among them."

EZEKIEL 2:3-6

However, Prophets, before you can do as God instructed Ezekiel, there are a few adjustments you need to make internally. Because, let's be honest, there have been several times when God gave you clearance to speak, but you remained silent. There have been countless instances where you *"heard God clearly"* but turned a deaf ear and acted like you hadn't heard anything at all. You didn't speak up because you were afraid they wouldn't listen. You didn't speak up because you were afraid to be ostracized by those you wanted to accept you. You didn't speak up because you were more fearful of not being invited to the next conference than you were of the repercussions that come with refusing to say what God said!

Let's make a few things abundantly clear.

1. The Prophet's office is not in place for those who occupy it to be liked.

Prophet, your assignment to David is to accurately hear the word of God and then, by the leading of the Holy

Spirit, release those words as unto a scalpel administering surgery upon the soul of that leader. Your assignment is to expose to David what may be invisible to him for the purpose of awareness, healing, transformation, and restoration. It is not your assignment to be liked, favored, or accepted by the king. You are already . . .

loved

favored

AND accepted

BY THE KING!

If you don't make that adjustment or fail to make that shift, you will NEVER fulfill your calling or assignment in the earth because you will lust after being liked instead of being a trusted oracle.

I hear your heart loud and clear. You know that things aren't being done with integrity. You see that David is behaving recklessly. You see the collateral damage that's being done. But you are still reluctant to say something to David. You are tired of being an outcast and living on the ministry margins. You want to be known as the one who delivers on stage but is still "*in touch with their humanity.*" You want to be one of the cool kids. Stop it. Stop begging God to send somebody else to do your task, Nathan! If God has spoken to you to speak to David, then you must do just that.

The Bible reveals the multitude of challenges that many prophets faced with a desire to not have to share strong words. They suffered with feeling that every time they came around, it was all doom and gloom. They dealt with being ostracized, singled out, and hated for obeying God. What you are experiencing isn't new. Every prophet before you dealt with it, and every prophet after you will deal with it. You can't help that every time you enter an area, demonic spirits get stirred up. I know it hurts to feel misunderstood, even without problematic speech. But conviction lives within your bones! It's not you... It's the office. And it's high time you made peace with that. It is vital that you get in the community of other prophets. If not, the isolation and rejection can be so heavy you will want to throw your scalpel away or, at the very least, not use it. Even worse, you may intentionally succumb to sin just to dull your blade!

2. There's NOTHING convenient about being a Prophet.

If you are going to walk out the fullness of being Nathan, you will be required to surrender your desires and aspirations. Many of you reading this have put down your Nathan assignment because it doesn't align with what and who you desire to be. The sad thing is, even though you've laid down the call, you still don't have peace. Do you want to know why? Because you aren't being who you were created to be. Nathan's role is, among many other things, a selfless role. You will wrestle DAILY with wanting to do your own thing. You will DAILY find yourself wondering, "What about my dreams, God? You will DAILY compromise personal desire for the sake of being obedient to God. But such is the woes of being a bona-fide Nathan. You exist for the purpose of bringing about a nonfiltered yet wisely communicated word, especially to those in leadership roles. If a word of safety can get to the head, then it can bring great protection to the body.

3. It's not your job to change them.

Many of Nathan's refuse to speak up because they think people won't listen. And if you do speak up, you only go as far as "You are the man." You are afraid that even if you put yourself out there and speak up when nobody else will, nothing will change except how they see YOU. Read this slowly:

YOU ARE <u>NOT</u> RESPONSIBLE FOR WHETHER THE WORD IS RECEIVED OR HEEDED.

It is the work of the Holy Spirit that convicts and brings about change. Your ONLY responsibility is to deliver the word. Stop mulling over the results of what God says, and SPEAK. You are ONLY the messenger. Stop looking for favorable results. Obeying God IS the favorable result.

4. Approach the leader in an honorable way.

Nathan, before you open your mouth to address anything, you need to pray. Many Nathans are FAILING in their assignments because as soon as they see something, they start speaking, murmuring, or gossiping, which can expose a leader God is trying to warn yet still cover. Whole networks of intercessors and prophets are moving demonically, sharing information in group threads and group messages, but nobody is praying. I understand that learning some not-so-favorable things about David can be so shocking, disappointing, and frustrating that your respect for David can begin to ween, but no matter what, you must always respect the role, especially if it's an office. Regardless of what God reveals to you or allows you to become privy to, you must quickly remember that your role is to ultimately HELP David. You can't do that if your actions are harming David. AND, many times, Prophets don't see to 'say.' They see to 'pray.' We cannot leave this out of the prophet's role in the life of a leader.

Finally, be prepared for when the king calls you up. Many times, God will give you insight into David and what he needs way ahead of time. God will speak things to you that you will only know by the Holy Spirit. God will show you how to rectify and redeem situations so that once David reaches out to you, you will be prepared to respond. Prayerfully seek God before engaging a leader. Before you are hopefully called up, bathe the prophetic word in prayer and ask God to deal with the leader's heart so they can receive what God has given you to share.

You can't help David if your actions are harming David.

In 2nd Samuel, Nathan didn't go blasting at David. The Lord sent Nathan to tell David a story first. You don't have to resort to instant aggression because you are a prophet. If you approach the leader, starting with "you are the man," you could miss what God wants you to do. Remember at all times that God's desire is always to redeem and restore.

Now, we're going to shift!
Take a breath!

Dear David (Senior Leader)

You may have been nodding and clapping as we discussed Nathan's role and the adjustments they need to make. However, you have a role to play as well. Let's start here. How open have you been to Nathan's role? Sure, at the beginning of your pastorate, you may have welcomed Nathan's insight. You were excited and thrilled to be in a new leadership position. You were so humbled to be the pastor and entrusted with the church. You saw Nathan as a help, an advisor, and somewhat of a guardrail. But what happened when you became more and more aware of the liberty your role provides? What happened when you realized the power of the loyalty people gave to you? What happened when you learned that you could do whatever you wanted and no one could check you about it because... you're the leader? What happened when you learned how to cover up your poor choices independently? What happened when you realized that, much like you, other leaders struggle with sin and are still pastoring pretty well without any accountability or desire for healing? *David, David, David.* What did being on the throne do to you?!

I'll tell you what it did.

It put the humility that was there at the genesis of your assignment underneath the enormous weight of access, opportunities, and the temptation that comes with high-level leadership. So now . . .

Nathan's help sounds like hindrances.
Nathan's advice sounds like assumptions.
And Nathan's guardrails sound like restraints.

You oppose everything Nathan says. When Nathan advises you to wait or slow down, you remind Nathan that you're the boss and you're in charge! Over time, you slowly exclude Nathan from important meetings. You diminish the authority you gave Nathan by talking about him or her with other leaders and members of the organization. You whisper that Nathan doesn't see the vision. And when Nathan finally musters up the courage to say, "*David, you are the man!*" you label Nathan as a witch/warlock or the all-time favorite, a Jezebel.

Now, you're running wild and free.

No one can check you. No one can call you to the carpet. No one can even give you a warning. You're surrounded by yes men & yes women who are willing to look the other way. When the repercussions of your hidden deeds finally surface and the statues you've built unto thine self finally come crashing down, you find yourself in a heap on the floor crying, "*God, why me?*"

All of which could have been prevented if you had allowed Nathan to serve you.

David, what you don't realize is that you really didn't *hire* Nathan. Nathan was sent by God's divine appointment to undergird you as you undershepherd his people. Nathan was not there for the genesis. Nathan was at the genesis so that he could support you in the middle, in the hopes that you won't have a premature end. Nathan is most needed when you become fixated on poorly exercising authority over who and what you lead. Nathan is not needed until you get into that season when you are at the crossroads of taking ungodly risks versus operating in righteousness. For it is at that critical juncture that your enemy can become your friend, and your friend can become your enemy if you're not prayerful.

David, you must wrestle against the temptation to push back your court of prophets at the very hour you need them the most. If you are beginning to feel agitation rise as you read about the necessity of Nathan, know that those could very well be demonic thoughts that desire you to fall for the tricks and schemes of the enemy. David, people are walking away from God because of your obsession with ambition. David, the sheep are scattered and anti-The Bride because of your misuse of authority. When will you wake up and realize that you NEED

> *Nathan is most needed when you become fixated on poorly exercising authority over who and what you lead.*

Nathan to maintain the right posture now that you are governing much?

Deal with Your Pride!

The biggest trick of the enemy is to pervert your view of God's protection. The concerns that you keep dismissing as correction are actually God's protection. Your sight can shift based on your height. The higher you go, the less clarity you may have. Your issue is you've gotten so high on the horse that no one can say anything to you. NO one can even offer you an opinion. Somewhere along the way, you started to believe that because *you're on the pulpit,* you can no longer be positively impacted *by the pew.* But you wanted it that way, right? That's why you got rid of the people who didn't always agree with you. That's why you removed the inquisitive and over-analytical, the people who would eventually ask enough questions to uncover what you work so hard to keep hidden. That's why you only elevate people who are so unclear on their identity that they look, sound, dress, act, and believe like you. You no longer have followers because you've replaced them with hundreds and thousands of clones. You publicly call these clones *sons and daughters*, mostly when they accomplish something that garners a lot of attention, but what the world doesn't know is that they can't even get

> *The biggest trick of the enemy is to pervert your view of God's protection.*

you on the phone. While we are here, let's go ahead and address the misuse and abuse of the beautiful concept of "honor." In many church cultures today, the word "honor" has been taken out of scriptural context and **used as a whip to keep sheep and supporting leaders in line.** Some leaders have brainwashed the congregations they're supposed to serve with a manipulative, incorrect doctrine of honor. Some leaders have blatantly and/or covertly made people believe that honor means never questioning, disagreeing, and/or feeling or thinking anything other than what the leader feels. Leaders have to become comfortable with those who follow them (especially those they've set in positions of leadership) being able to offer up respectful questions. Newsflash:

To disagree does not equal dishonor.

Leader, if this has been you, please allow God to circumcise your heart and address pride so that you can stop derailing every attempt God makes to protect your life and the lives of those who follow you.

"First pride, then the crash - the bigger the ego, the harder the fall."

PROVERBS 16:18

Free Yourself of Embarrassment and Shame.

When we feel shame, our first response is to hide ourselves, someone, or something. Take a look at what Adam did in the Garden of Eden. He sowed up some fig leaves to hide his nakedness (his pure form) from God. Why did Adam hide himself? For the same reason you hide, David. Shame is the painful feeling of humiliation or distress caused by the consciousness of wrong behavior. This means that someone expressing your flaws forces into reality the very thing you pushed into your unconsciousness. Shame keeps us from wanting our flaws to be revealed, but it also keeps us from being able to heal. You cannot heal what you refuse to reveal. David, I understand the magnitude of your flaws may be great, but despite your previous efforts, you cannot fix them by yourself. The beautiful thing is, you don't have to. You need to be open to God sending you help through a Nathan. Deal with your shame head-on. Stop hiding your flaws. Process how you got here, then do the work to transcend. Stop pushing Nathan away. The breakthrough you need is on the other side of your willingness to let in a prophetic light.

Shame keeps us from wanting our flaws to be revealed, but it also keeps us being able to heal.

Repent

The bottom line is, David, your leadership should never get to a point where Nathan has to come in and declare, "*You are the man!*" Once this is required, there is a dead Uriah and a baby, and people's lives will now be greatly impacted by your actions. People are already bleeding by that point. Leader, God wants you to constantly evaluate your own heart and emotions so that it is unnecessary for Nathan to have to come with such a strong rebuke. It doesn't matter how anointed you believe you are. What do you need to put in place to ensure you have accountability? Who do you have in place to reflect YOU back to YOU? It is not God's intention for people's interaction with you to cause them harm. God entrusted you to feed His sheep and help them grow.

I am fully aware that this chapter may have been more challenging than the others. But keep in mind that God chastens those that He loves. David, this chapter is God's attempt to get your attention. Wherever you find yourself at this very moment, whether you are reading these words on a flight in the air, in your office at the church, or your bedroom at home, you can take a moment right now to repent. Let's not go into the next section without repenting to God and declaring that because He trusted us in these spiritual positions, we will do whatever we can to show ourselves worthy of the trusted role.

If you're willing and ready to repent,
you can pray the following...

Eternal God,

I come to you as the undershepherd that you entrusted to care for your sheep. My eyes of understanding have been opened to see some errors I have made along my journey thus far. It was never my intention to harm but to help. As I am still processing how I got to this space, I am compelled to repent and ask for your forgiveness and grace to be applied unto me. Help me to lead in a manner that brings you glory & restore me to a place of honor before you and the people I'm called to serve.

In Jesus' Name, Amen.

Chapter Six

GO SOMEWHERE AND SIT DOWN!

"**A Psalm of David.** *The LORD is my Shepherd [to feed, to guide and to shield me], I shall not want. He lets me lie down in green pastures; He leads me beside the still and quiet waters. He refreshes and restores my soul (life).*"

PSALM 23:1-3A

Leadership demands the need for a multiplicity of tools, such as wisdom, discipline, discernment, and effective communication, just to name a few. However, in my counsel with leaders, I have found that absent from their arsenal is a tool critical to their success, as well as the success of that in which they lead. That tool is called **REST**. Rest is defined as ceasing work or movement in order to relax, refresh, restore oneself, or recover strength. When most people hear or read the word rest, it often has a passive inclination. However, rest is a verb, an action word. Though, at times, rest can feel passive, what it produces is powerfully active. From that understanding, I have coined the phrase, *The Supernatural Power of Rest.*

ME TOO!

"The LORD is my Shepherd [to feed, to guide and to shield me], I shall not want."

PSALM 23:1-2

In Chapter Four, Still Sheep, we explored the duality of our personal lives versus our callings. Thus, we are embracing that though at times we are undershepherds, we are also still sheep. This chapter is designed for the soul of the sheep in order to preserve the undershepherd. Only from a sheep space can you utter the words, "*The Lord is my Shepherd.*" You enter into this chapter acknowledging, as David did in Psalm 23, that I, too, need to be fed. I, too, need to be guided. And I, too, need to be shielded.

Rest has the supernatural power to guide, feed, and protect.

Sheep leader, the Lord wants to shepherd you through this chapter. It is the Lord's intention to show you a portion of your life that could be lacking. What you may not have known is that rest has the supernatural power to guide. Rest has the supernatural power to feed. Rest can be a canopy of shielded protection. Therefore, you, leader, cannot afford to cast another vision, host another conference, or hire another team member until you have submitted to the supernatural power of rest.

LIE DOWN

"*He maketh me to lie down in green pastures.*"

PSALM 23:2

Leader, can I ask you a question? Has God been trying to lay you down? Have things been occurring in your life that have been loud beckonings for you to rest? In the King James Version, the second verse of Psalm 23 says, "He **MAKETH** me to lie down." Do you intend to answer the call to rest? Or are you determined to force God's hands to *maketh* you lie down?

That headache is your *maketh* call.
The unshakeable sadness is your *maketh* call.
Your unrelenting anxiety is your *maketh* call.

Let's not stop there.

<u>Your children's</u> headache is your *maketh* call.
<u>Your spouse's</u> unshakeable sadness is your *maketh* call.
<u>Your team's</u> unrelenting anxiety is your *maketh* call.

I pray that this chapter causes you to choose rest instead of having to acquiesce to a forced (maketh) rest.

IT'S OKAY TO BE STILL

"*He leads me beside the still and quiet waters. He refreshes and restores my soul (life);*"

PSALM 23:2-3A

We often use noise as a panacea to the noise occurring in our souls. To drown out the cries of our emotions, we choose to live in pools of turbulent and loud water. We use noise to run from what's going on in our souls. We run to dysfunctional environments to avoid the confusion within. When things get too quiet, our lives are brought before us. Reality hits, and we realize that what we deemed safe may not be so safe... and what we labeled well may not be so well. So, the real question is:

Are you truly that busy? Or, are you using the busyness of your schedule as a bandage for your gaping wounds?

Leader, what you need is consistent, weekly times of stillness and quietness. In the belly of pools of peace, your mind and emotions can be refreshed and then restored. You need to rest to live! The Bible gives us the prescription for ensuring that we are consistently resting.

"*Observe the Sabbath day by keeping it holy as the Lord your God has commanded you. Six days you shall labor and do all your work, but one day out of the week, I want that to be our day. On it, I don't want you to do any work.*"

DEUTERONOMY 5:12-15

Every six days, your body is wired to need to pause from activity. Our bodies are almost like a machine, and they need to have consistent opportunities to power down. This one day a week does not have to be a Saturday; *it can be any day you desire.* Pray about choosing one day out of each week to cease striving.

Sabbath resting is not about sitting in a corner Indian style, rocking back and forth, and meditating. That's not how Sabbath rest has to look. God is saying, "*I want there to be one day where you don't have pressure. I want there to be one day where you move effortlessly and laugh uncontrollably. Whatever you do is fine as long as what you do brings you pure joy.*" Weekly Sabbath rest will increase you in three areas:

- Your spiritual discernment
- Your spiritual awareness
- Your spiritual effectiveness

Leader, if you think you are productive now, wait until you get into the habit of resting one day a week. You will be amazed at what you can produce within a rested vessel. Once you make your Sabbath day mandatory, what you accomplish in the other six days will be supernaturally powerful.

"If you watch your step on the Sabbath, that one day a week, and don't use that day for personal advantage. If you treat the day as a day of joy, God's day of celebration, if you honor it by refusing business as usual, making money. Running here and there, then you'll be free to enjoy God. I'll make you ride high and soar above it all."

Isaiah 58:13-14

What's important to highlight is that there are multiple layers to rest. There is spiritual, physical, intellectual, and emotional rest. I think it would be helpful to expound upon each one individually.

SPIRITUAL REST

It is impossible to rest our physical bodies if our spirits are ill at ease. Have you ever had something really bother or weigh on your spirit? Even after wrestling with that thing all day, you still can't shake it off. So you take a good hot shower, get into a bed with fresh, clean sheets, and turn off the lights. Unfortunately, even though the environment is perfectly set, you still can't seem to fall off to sleep. If you've ever wondered why, it's because when your spirit is ill at ease, your body will follow suit. So God says primarily, "*You must have rest for your spirit before you can experience rest for your body.*" The greatest result of Sabbath rest is the opportunity for your spirit to rest in the presence of God.

> *Sabbath rest grants our spirit the opportunity to rest in the presencce of God.*

The challenge with spiritual resting is that it requires utter and complete trust in God. Leader, when your spirit is not at ease about something, you can be sure you are not completely trusting God in that area. Now, let's *take a deep breath* here because we're going to take a bit of a turn now. I need you to grasp this so that your spiritual rest can be fulfilling. When you fully trust God in an area, it doesn't matter what your present circumstances might be. You realize that you don't need to rely on your strength to endure because God's strength is truly enough. If you are up in the middle of the night and cannot sleep, you are not allowing God to be God. Rather than continue to toss and turn until daybreak, recognize that you are not allowing God to Lord over the situation that's robbing you of rest. Admit that there's something in you questioning if God's strong enough. Admit that your past is haunting you and suggesting that you don't deserve what you may be in need of. Admit that you, the pastor, are struggling to believe that God loves you enough to work the situation out for your good.

If you are restless, you are not allowing God to Lord over the situation.

Spiritual rest grants us the freedom to accept that human happiness is fleeting. It allows us to sit in the presence of God, embrace joy, and trust that His grace is enough to carry us through divers trials. Yes, leader, you will experience difficult times, but our faith assures us that God is with us in our difficult times.

If God is with us, despite what is going on, there is an ending and an exit to this situation.

It's going to be good on the other side of this, but greater than that, you'll be the better on the other side of this.

Let your spirit REST.

PHYSICAL REST

The Sabbath is never a day to allow ourselves to be pushed into an activity, especially by our own false guilt or other's expectations. If we cannot rest one day a week, we take ourselves far too seriously. Leader, you're not that important.

The job will continue to move forward.
The church will still hold services.
The usher board will still be able to usher.
Everything will be okay if you take some time away.

Previous generations perpetuated the notion, "*I can't take a day because they need me.*" As a result, young adults were not properly groomed for the next generation, and many an endeavor, organization, and edifice have crumbled due to leaders' inability to properly gauge when their presence is required and when it can just momentarily expire.

Leader, let's be clear. I know you'd like to label your incessant busyness and unrelenting work ethic as faithfulness. But that's not always the case. Sometimes, it's pride. Therefore, no, it is not a time management issue. No, it's not a lack of reliable staff issue. Your challenge is that you think if it's not done by your hands, then you'll lose some sort of positional footing and amassed power gained through commendable productivity.

This is what I suggest you do. Fully examine your weeks. Find tasks that can be done by others. Find time slots that can be minimized or rerouted. And make a deliberate decision to ensure your temple gets weekly consistent physical rest. Leader, I challenge you to delegate. I challenge you to ask for and accept help. I challenge you to stop making your roles, tasks, and titles an idol. I challenge you to cease believing that you are what you do! The truth is, leader, you are so much greater than your accomplished tasks. Allow yourself and others to love you for YOU!

Take a deep breath in. . .

Now release. . .

Let's continue. . .

INTELLECTUAL REST

Intellectual rest is vital for those with analytical minds. We tend to be the most troubled when it comes to rest. In the silence of our Sabbath times, our minds can rest, lending the freedom to learn anew how best to use our minds to the glory of God. Ceasing from labor and resting our brains dispels the frenzied fear that drives our minds when we fall prey to the world's expectations for constant accomplishment. In addition, our intellectual rest gives us the courage to give up any senseless thinking or intellectual pride that might thwart God's promises.

You think you need to be awake to find the answer to the solution. God says, "*If you go somewhere and sit down, I'll reveal the strategy.*" Your intellect may not be as immense as you imagine it to be. It's also probable that your intelligence is the culprit. It could be getting in the way of the magnitude of the creativity and the blueprint God wants to download. The solution might be on the creative side of your brain, which is why God is like, "*I just want you to go to the beach, lay out, and drink a pina colada...without rum.*" Sometimes, it's not your intellect that's gonna get the job done. It's God's intellect. But God can't give you His mind if you're determined that everything be birthed out of yours.

> *Your intelligence may be getting in the way of the creativity God wants to deposit in you.*

EMOTIONAL REST

There's a story in 1 Kings 19 that really displays beautifully the importance of emotional rest. In this story, we see a biblical character by the name of Elijah. In the previous chapter (chapter 18), we had just seen Elijah come through on the other side of a major battle on behalf of God. God came through in a very powerful way and showed everybody that He is who He says He is, an all-powerful God. So one would think that Elijah, after having God come through and show Himself mighty and strong, would be excited and celebrate a victory against the Prophets of Baal. But we see something very different happen within Elijah's emotions. He was undoubtedly excited, but we also witnessed him have great trepidation. He was relieved yet overwhelmed by what this victory would subsequently mean. He felt fear with exhilaration; terror, along with confidence.

This leads us to pose these questions: How can we accomplish a great feat and still doubt ourselves? How does God use us mightily when we minister, but when we return to our office, home, or hotel, we feel worse than when we began? It was so emotionally plaguing for Elijah that the Bible says he wanted to die.

"Now Ahab told Jezebel all that Elijah had done, and how he had killed all the prophets [of Baal] with the sword. Then Jezebel sent a messenger to Elijah, saying, "So may the gods do to me, and even more, if by this time tomorrow I do not make your life like the life of one of them." And Elijah was afraid and arose and ran for his life, and he came to Beersheba which belongs to Judah, and he left his servant there. But he himself traveled a day's journey into the wilderness, and he came and sat down under a juniper tree and asked [God] that he might die."

1 KINGS 19:1-4

The Bible says when he came to Beersheba and Judah, he left his servant there while he went on a day's journey into the wilderness. He came to a broom bush. Sat down under it and prayed that he might die. That's suicidal ideation right in the text after a major accomplishment.

How can someone get to the point where the flood of a multiplicity of emotions causes them to not even want to live? It's a vessel that has been robbed of consistent emotional rest. Elijah was emotionally exhausted. And I want to suggest that it wasn't solely from his most recent battle but from a lack of emotional rest over 18 previous chapters. So, let's see what God's prescription was for this prophet because it's the same prescription He has for us:

"He lay down and slept under the juniper tree, and behold, an angel touched him and said to him, "Get up and eat." He looked, and by his head there was a bread cake baked on hot coal, and a pitcher of water. So he ate and drank and lay down again. Then the angel of the Lord came again a second time and touched him and said, "Get up, and eat, for the journey is too long for you [without adequate sustenance]." So he got up and ate and drank, and with the strength of that food he traveled forty days and nights to Horeb (Sinai), the mountain of God."

1 KINGS 19:5-8

God's prescription was for Elijah to lay down and rest. Rest was the manner in which God decided to settle, organize, sort through, and strengthen Elijah's emotions. Mind you, all of this would be occurring not BY Elijah but within Elijah, supernaturally, as he rested. But notice that not only did he rest, but he was refueled after coming out of that rest, and this occurred not once but TWICE! Through this rest, God not only restored Elijah from his previous battle, but God also fueled Elijah for his future battle. Rest is God's way of ensuring our vitality and longevity. For those in leadership capacities, you cannot afford to just rest or replenish once. It must be a consistent discipline that you begin to see value in. It's a strategic spiritual warfare tool not just against your adversaries but to armor your soul.

While you are serving the world, your soul still matters to God. It is God's ultimate desire that many people are healed through your gifts poured out, however, God also has the power to keep you whole along the journey. Was Jesus, in many ways, a wounded healer? Yes! We do, however, need to grapple with whether theologically we are called to do the same. I believe that we have begun to wear emotional dysfunction as a badge of Spiritual honor, instead of being sober on what afflictions are truly God-ordained versus situational and generationally maintained. We may need to finally release the emotional weights God never intended for us to carry. Rest is a major way to lay every false burden down.

> *While you are serving the world, your soul still matters to God.*

God says, "*I want you to slow down so you can sense me. I want you to slow down so you can feel me. I want you to slow down so you can hear me. I want you to slow down so you can see me. I want you to slow down so that you can trust me. I want you to slow down so you can follow me. I want you to slow down so that you can rest in me, and I want you to slow down so that you can live for me.*" In order to keep standing, you have to keep sitting. So . . .

Go somewhere and sit down.

Chapter Seven

IT'S NOT PERSONAL, IT'S ETHICAL

Leader, in the previous chapters, we walked through many challenging conversations to ensure that you are emotionally well enough to carry out the assignment God has given you. In our final chapter, I will provide you with a code of ethics to maintain your health and integrity and that of the ministries you lead.

Many vocations have made it a necessity to intentionally govern their standard of conduct and optimal operation with guiding principles known as an organization's code of ethics. Ethics is defined as a set of moral principles, especially ones related to or confirming the boundaries of a specified group or form of personal conduct. In these various vocations, the code of ethics is a guiding light, or a North Star if you will, to keep everyone under its canopy mindful of the conduct necessary to do the greatest good and the least harm.

Medical, law enforcement, financial, and even political professions, just to name a few, have all years ago established their own code of ethics. In writing this book, I was shocked to discover that Christian clergy do not have an official overarching code of ethics. In my professional assessment, many challenges have arisen in Christendom because we have been unclear about what should be our guiding ethics.

"Do not conform to the pattern of this world, but be transformed by the renewing of your mind. Then, you will be able to test and approve what God's will is – his good, pleasing, and perfect will."

ROMANS 12:2

In addition to a compromised emotional well-being, some Christian clergy are moving unethically because we don't have defined morals that govern how we carry out ministry. Despite having the Bible as our ultimate North Star, our many denominations, doctrines, and interpretations of our sacred text have lended to discourse among clergy about what is and is not acceptable. However, ethics is not an issue of doctrine, denomination, or interpretation. You can choose not to believe in The Holy Trinity, but if you don't believe in the dignity and worth of people beyond being a good leader, it may be necessary to consider if you are a good human being. Ethics is simply about *whether your existence does good in the world or causes harm.*

Complaining about what is absent is futile when a solution can be offered. To that end, I humbly suggest the following ethics be adopted by those who serve in the sacred capacity of ecclesial servant leadership...

1
SERVANTHOOD

Ministry Servant Leaders must consistently keep at the forefront that the Bible is clear that "The greatest among you shall be your servant." (Matthew 23:11). We are charged with the care and aid of those who follow our leadership. Therefore, those who carry greatness will show greatness, not in asserting dominance, but in a life of servanthood.

To fully grasp and apply the principle Jesus gives us in Matthew 23:11, we must accept that the Kingdom of God operates completely different from our culture and society. In the Kingdom...

We RECEIVE by GIVING

"Give, and it will be given to you. A good measure, pressed down, shaken together, and running over, will be poured into your lap. For with the measure you use, it will be measured to you."

LUKE 6:38

We GAIN LIFE by GIVING UP OUR LIFE

"Whoever finds his life will lose it, and whoever loses his life for my sake will find it."

MATTHEW 10:39

We become STRONG when we are WEAK.

"But he said to me, "My grace is sufficient for you, for my power is made perfect in weakness." Therefore I will boast all the more gladly about my weaknesses, so that Christ's power may rest on me. That is why, for Christ's sake, I delight in weaknesses, in insults, in hardships, in persecutions, in difficulties. For when I am weak, then I am strong."

2 CORINTHIANS 12:9-10

In Luke 9, there arose a dispute among the disciples about who was considered the greatest, which Jesus settles by exposing yet another "*upside down*" principle of the Kingdom of God. In our culture, historically, the greatest are those that have servants. However, the Kingdom, as it does in many areas, invites us into a complete shift in mindset. The greatest among us aren't those who are served but rather those who serve. As servant leaders, we must ask ourselves:

Are our efforts driven by a lust to be served or our desire to serve?

Failure to grasp the concept of being servants has caused many ministries' pursuits to be of no effect. Clamoring for prestige can make our ministry pursuits empty, however, when we serve without selfish motives and vain ambition, we can accomplish great things for the Glory of God.

2
DIGNITY & WORTH OF ALL PEOPLE

Ministry Servant Leaders respect the inherent dignity and worth of all people. We are called to treat each person we encounter in a caring and respectful fashion. We are mindful that regardless of one's circumstances, socioeconomic status, cultural differences, or beliefs, people deserve to be treated with respect.

Those we serve...

As Ministry Servant Leaders, we deal with people who have or are currently experiencing, a myriad of challenges. We will most likely intersect with them at a season of uncertainty, fracture, limitation, and/or social, emotional, or spiritual trauma. Their varying life experiences to date could have landed them in tremendous need, placing them in a season of deficit. So, regardless of how fragile they may be in the season we meet them, it is critical they be treated with respect and dignity.

Those we serve alongside...

About twenty years ago, a trend began amongst clergy, silently separating those deemed worthy and those who were not. This trend has increased with the advancement of technology and the quickly growing impact of social media. It has been a consistent part of human nature to be attracted to, drawn to, or want to aspire to those who demonstrate wealth, status, and popularity. With that, we must be mindful to ensure that those individuals are not the only ones given kindness, thought, and consideration.

As a sociologist who studies human behavior and its overarching impact on societal relations, I have found that some ministry leaders, especially senior leaders, tend to only be kind to people who are further educationally or experientially than them, have crossed into an upper-class tax bracket, or have social media status (usually decided based on how many followers the person has accumulated). In 15 years of speaking on the road across the country, I have watched how senior leaders' appearance of kindness is predicated on who's in the room and is only given to those with the resources to help them ascend a perceived ladder of success. This needs to cease.

The lust and obsession with ambition cause clergy to not see the dignity in those they serve, the dignity amongst their colleagues, and even, at times, the dignity of those who have gone before them. This obsession with ambition usually comes from unaddressed emotional deficits from a root of a diminished or non-cultivated sense of true self-worth. An obsession with ambition can prevent a ministry servant leader from walking out this entire code of ethics. Why? **Obsession causes a preoccupation with fruitless vanishing gains.** It's challenging to be insightful or thoughtful if you are nursing a persistent, disturbing preoccupation with self-aggrandizement. The Bible offers us this caution...

"Do nothing out of selfish ambition or vain conceit. Rather, in humility value others above yourselves."

PHILIPPIANS 2:3

I do want to be clear that God-given wealth and influence are beautiful blessings that God trusts us to steward in a manner that brings Him glory. There are people that God graces with enormous financial surplus and influence for the purpose of kingdom impact and to advance the will of God in the earth. If you are one of those individuals, guard against the temptation to begin lusting after power, wealth, or influence to the point where it causes you to discount the value and worth of those who seemingly have nothing to offer you.

If you don't consistently see the dignity and worth in all people, you will eventually be unable to see the value in serving them.

3
SOCIAL JUSTICE

Ministry Servant Leaders are called to exhibit empathy and sensitivity to ethnically diverse populations and to assist and come alongside their efforts to combat oppression. We are tasked with the courage to take on issues of social injustice on behalf of those who are marginalized due to circumstances beyond their control.

Jesus' heart was always turned towards the marginalized. Those who found themselves, of no choice or fault of their own, being seen in society as less than or unworthy of human decency found the compassion they needed from Jesus. As ministers, we are charged to be mindful of and advocate for the rights of those whose voices, cultural biases, and pride have attempted to silence. We speak up, and when needed, we show up with an inherent belief that we're not truly free if others are bound.

"Learn to do well; seek judgment, relieve the oppressed, judge the fatherless, plead for the widow."

ISAIAH 1:17

"This is what the LORD of Heaven's Armies says: Judge fairly, and show mercy and kindness to one another. Do not oppress widows, orphans, foreigners, and the poor. And do not scheme against each other."

ZECHARIAH 7:9-10

"Do you know what I want? I want justice—oceans of it. I want fairness—rivers of it. That's what I want. That's all I want."

AMOS 5:24

4
SEXUAL RELATIONSHIPS

Ministry Servant Leaders should avoid sexual activity with those whom they are in authority over. There is a clear power dynamic that infringes on the ability for the relationship to be experienced by either party from an equal and sober place.

It is without question that the sexual aspects of who we are as human beings have not been properly explored nor discussed from a theological perspective within the church. Sexual intimacy is a powerful experience designed by God to create beauty out of a seed of love. As with anything that possesses power, boundaries, and guardrails become critical. When a person has met someone and submitted to their oversight or authority, the relationship creates an instant power dynamic that includes a desire to please coupled with a reluctance to deny. These dynamics can render both the authority figure and those submitted to their leadership incapable, at times, of filtering their experiences in a manner healthy for the dynamics of romantic engagement.

As a leader, it is important to be cognizant of why something is occurring. While you may believe that someone's sexual interest is directly connected to their desire for you, they could be attempting to satisfy you in an effort to satisfy their selfish ambition. Or, their aim may be to increase how others view them (and how they view themselves) by attaching themselves to your position of power and influence.

Even more frightening, if they are stunted in their early childhood development, they could be attempting to fill their void of parental love and care through their sexual advances towards you. They don't truly desire you as a sexual partner, they want you to be the father or mother they never had. There's a fine line between sexual intimacy and parental intimacy that gets its genesis in early childhood development. If that fine line is not properly stewarded, it can become sexual dysfunction.

If you currently find yourself in a relationship that has one or both of the two previous dynamics shared, I strongly suggest that you end that relationship. While you may feel a strong attachment to them, no matter what you put on top of it, if the foundation isn't pure, the fruit will be tainted. God doesn't want that for them or you.

5
CONFIDENTIALITY

Ministry Servant Leaders should possess the ability to honor and, therefore, keep private all information that is shared with them in confidence or that their position may warrant them being aware of that is sensitive in nature. The clergy's role must remain trustworthy and safe. Therefore, the keeping or management of privacy must be paramount. Under the banner of being a mandated reporter (which all licensed clergy are), confidentiality should be broken only in the case of suicidal or homicidal ideation and any sexual occurrences with a minor or non-consenting adult. In those instances, the family, the intended victim, and/or the authorities should be notified immediately.

The clergy role is a trusted role. Many assume that when they share information and/or seek counsel from a ministry leader, that information will be kept private. The nature of information shared with a leader, either by other leaders within their organization or by members of said organization, is often sensitive in nature. When a leader chooses to break the sacred trust of confidentiality, the one who shared the information becomes vulnerable. Such breaches of trust also cause unnecessary fear, doubt, or apprehension within the leadership team as well as the congregation. Many implosions of ecclesial culture have occurred through the bombs of breached trust. Herein lies a poignant example of the need for healthy, mature emotional leadership. The younger someone is in emotional age, the more difficult it is for them to *hold it*.

I encourage leaders to simply adopt the concept that if it's not your story to tell, don't tell it. The person permitted you to hear it, not to spread it.

"Whoever goes about slandering reveals secrets, but he who is trustworthy in spirit keeps a thing covered."

PROVERBS 11:13

6
ACCOUNTABILITY

Ministry servant leaders benefit from willingly submitting to accountability. As a metaphoric umbrella, accountability can be a layer of covering and protection. Accountability should flow in three directions: the benefit of having a pastor/spiritual leader, the support and sounding board that comes from trusted colleagues, and the humility that comes from being accountable to those you serve.

Accountability to spiritual leaders...

Most people, if they see that it is raining outside, will grab an umbrella so they don't get wet. They are trying to ensure that the elements they cannot control don't have the ability to directly impact them in a way that would cause them to become sick and, therefore, unwell for a season to perform their duties. It's great that we do that when it is raining, however, I encourage you to be the type of person that ensures they have an umbrella with them at all times. Be the type of person that may keep one in their bag, car, or office because they understand that though when they first started the day, the skies were clear, there is still a possibility that an unexpected storm may arise. It is the same way when it comes to the power of submitting to a covering, which is what accountability does.

As much as we may already know, there is much more to be known. It takes a level of humility to recognize that we should always be evolving and that we all have blind spots. A pastor or spiritual advisor should be able to provide you wise counsel on your journey. You want someone in your corner who has successfully walked the road you are currently walking. If they have, there is a high probability that they are aware of future pitfalls. It is the hope that your covering has mastered moving through your context's terrain and has a knowledge of circumstances that no academic textbook can properly prepare you for. In addition to situational awareness, it's a benefit to you that they know YOU and see YOU -- your strengths and areas of growth. While we are prone to want to hide our imperfections, a good covering will provide an atmosphere of safety that will encourage you to be vulnerable so that you do not become vulnerable to attack.

Accountability to colleagues...

The second direction of accountability can be experienced through the horizontal connection between you and trusted colleagues. There is a well-known phrase that says, "I am my brother's keeper." It is in trusted spaces that we can become aware of our blind spots. Our horizontal connections provide a level of comfort that strips us of any apprehension to emotionally undress. In these sacred connections, redirection can occur with the least amount of collateral damage. At this level, not only can you be the recipient, but you can also be a source of accountability to others. Many times, we receive insight, clarity, and even answers as we are being a source of support to someone else. God has not designed us to live our lives in isolation. If you haven't already, I encourage you to pray and open your heart to God sending these relationships into your life.

Accountability to those we serve...

The third direction of accountability occurs when we have the humility to submit to those we serve. There is a power and peace that comes with a willingness to offer God-led transparency to those who have trusted to follow our leadership. Trust is something that remains intact through the method of communication. Giving an account through communication of where things stand can provide great incentive to follow your leadership.

7
CHARACTER

Ministry Servant Leaders should be principled, sincere, and fair. It should be our aim to choose the highest, most Christ-like choice, even if that choice may be difficult or cause discomfort for ourselves or others. We choose to take responsibility for our actions without displacing. We are free of corruption and hypocrisy in speech and deed, in both public and private spaces.

"A good name [earned by honorable behavior, godly wisdom, moral courage, and personal integrity] is more desirable than great riches."

PROVERBS 22:1A

There is a well-known phrase that says, "*All you have is your name.*" It's a phrase used throughout history to encourage someone to see the value in their reputation. A person's character speaks to whether they can be trusted and respected. While we give honor to spiritual offices because of the impact that the offices are designed to have in the earth, we must understand that a lack of character can only hide for so long behind the respect of the office.

It takes conscious, intentional choices daily to do what is right in the eyes of God. It is not lost on me how easy it is to slip into speech and/or actions that would be questionable. However, the same effort and diligence placed upon our outward presentations must be equally placed upon our private or inward decisions. If we refuse to do so, a lack of character will inevitably cause us to be stripped of trust and our opportunities to offer public presentations.

Without conscious awareness, we can fall into the trap of believing that one inappropriate statement, action, or choice has no impact outside the specific moment. However, the enemy is banking on this lack of attentiveness so that we never become sober and realize we are living two different lives. Therefore, it should be our perpetual aim to choose to be forthright in our confessions and transactions, enabling us to live above board and not duplicitous.

What's done in the dark will eventually come to light, and when you're a leader, that exposure will not just impact you, it will impact everyone connected to you. This is so important to God that the Bible speaks to it on multiple occasions...

"For nothing is secret, that shall not be made manifest; neither any thing hid, that shall not be known and come abroad."

LUKE 8:17

"But there is nothing [so carefully] concealed that it will not be revealed, nor so hidden that it will not be made known. For that reason, whatever you have said in the dark will be heard in the light, and what you have whispered behind closed doors will be proclaimed on the housetops."

LUKE 12:2

"Show yourself in all respects to be a model of good works, and in your teaching show integrity, dignity, and sound speech that cannot be condemned, so that an opponent may be put to shame, having nothing evil to say about us."

TITUS 2:7-8

8
EMOTIONAL HEALTH

Ministry Servant Leaders must keep at the forefront that "you can teach and preach out of what you know, but you can only lead out of who you are" {Pete Scazzero}. As emotions can impact decisions, how we manage the emotional components of who we are can make or break our leadership. Seeking out various forms of counseling can prove to be advantageous regarding any unaddressed soul wounds, as well as assisting with the maintenance of existing wellness.

"Beloved, I pray that in every way you may prosper and enjoy good health, as your soul also prospers."

JOHN 3:1-2

So much of our life's traffic occurs on the highway of our soul. While we cannot see emotions physically, they have a tremendous impact on both natural and spiritual interactions. Our emotions become a filter through which we view ourselves, the world around us, and how we process information and experiences. If aspects of our emotional health are compromised, we may fall prey to decisions and behaviors that are harmful to ourselves and others.

Ministry leadership cannot be successfully administered by someone who is emotionally stunted.

You cannot be spiritually mature while remaining an emotional infant. Allowing yourself room to soberly view and receive healing is something you deserve and are worthy of. While historically, therapeutic interventions have not always been viewed in a favorable light, we need to cease our reluctance to see a difference between our emotional and physical health. Many of the diseases (dis-eases) that appear in our physical bodies have their origins in unaddressed traumas of the soul. But as soon as you work it out emotionally, it can be sorted out physically.

I hope that, if nothing else, this literary offering has deposited a seed within you to seek professional support from a licensed clinical therapist so that you can experience the wellness you deserve. What happened to you does not have to continue to control you. Silence is not power. Healing is power. You can only lead people into healing as far as you have been made well.

9
PHYSICAL HEALTH

Ministry Servant Leaders are cognizant that in many instances, they are the tool. There is significant physical exertion used in Ministry Moments, especially in teaching & preaching. Intentionality in getting weekly physical exercise is critical to ensuring endurance, stamina, and mental clarity. Movement is medicine.

"Or do you not know that your body is a temple of the Holy Spirit within you, whom you have from God? You are not your own, for you were bought with a price. So glorify God in your body."

1 Corinthians 6:19-20 ESV

While some vocations use a multiplicity of concrete tools to produce their desired results, ministry servant leaders' primary tool, after the Bible, is our literal bodies. We speak, teach, and preach through our bodies. These activities can really take a toll on us physically. In the same way we would consider the consistent maintenance of a vehicle used to transport its passengers from one place to another, we must do the same with our physical bodies. The very concrete need for eight hours of sleep daily, water consistently, eating a clean diet, and the understanding that physical exercise can bring healing to all aspects of who we are is critical. There are already great battles built into our assignment. Spiritual warfare is par for the course. With that in mind, let's not add to the things that are already in opposition to us walking out our calling. We must be first partakers of the wellness we want the people to receive.

10
COMPETENCE

Ministry Servant Leaders should only operate within their current level of competency. We should pursue continuous higher education and ministry development training so that we can perform our duties at the highest level required. All senior ministry leaders should possess both a bachelor's degree and a Master of Divinity or Biblical Studies degree.

Certain professions have within them the ability to greatly help and greatly harm. These professions are nuanced, layered, and meticulous. These professions have such an enormous complexity that they demand extensive intellectual preparation. There is not one ministry servant leader that, if they had a medical challenge with their heart, thus needing to be seen by a cardiologist, would choose one that had never been to school. In actuality, there would be no option to choose a cardiologist who had not been to school. We as clergy leaders must assess why there is even dialogue about whether or not academic education is necessary for our praxis.

As I have sat and pondered on why there is debate within the canopy of competency, one thing I have deduced is that because our profession is led by something unseen, moved through a kingdom system that is unseen, and produces results that often start in a realm that is unseen, we have been hiding behind the spirit world.

Maybe you need an example...

Once a high worship experience concludes, how would we create a written diagnostic that proves that one person's heart was convicted, that another came to the end of their need to be angry, that another person's unforgiveness was pulled down, and that another person had a change of mind? We have been operating heavy machinery, though invisible to the naked eye, and because God is a mystery, we have chosen to be lazy in our willingness to pursue scholastic understanding of God and His ways.

While medical physicians are discovering things about the mystery of the human body daily, you still would not lay on a table and allow someone to physically cut you open had they not spent a specific amount of time studying something so beautifully complex. If years of study are necessary to learn how to handle a physical body, then years of study must be VITAL to learn how to handle a spiritual body.

I know you may feel that you have a *natural ability,* but you need to learn how to appropriately steward that ability. If our manual (The Bible) is loaded, coded, and full of beautiful metaphor/symbolism, then you will do nothing but benefit from the intentional, guided study so that people don't have to continue to sit inside your eisegesis when their freedom comes from proper exegesis.

It is not by happenstance that we've concluded this chapter dealing with competence last. While competence is extremely important, it pales in comparison to the previous nine suggested ethics that we covered. This book has been about highlighting the importance of an aspect of ourselves that is invisible to the eye but can be greatly experienced by the body, and that aspect is our emotional well-being. We have to shift our attention away from what can clearly be seen, to the invisible components of who we are that can be clearly experienced. Many leaders are being haunted by an invisible source, and I want to suggest that it's your wounded soul begging for recourse.

When the HEAD HURTS, *the body keeps the score.*
When the HEAD HURTS, *the body becomes sore.*
When the HEAD HURTS, *the body*
is going to follow suit.
When the HEAD HURTS, *it's time*
to examine its root.

I sincerely pray that as you've read this book, many things have come to the surface. I pray you were confronted with some current truths and experienced God's hand of loving rebuke. God wants to heal every hurt you possess so that you, too, can drink from the fountain of wellness that you've sacrificed your life to lead others to!

Leader, wellness is not just for the Body;
it's for the HEAD, too!

I'm praying for you!

ABOUT THE AUTHOR

Dr. Khaalida Forbes, a native of New York, holds a Bachelor of Arts degree in Sociology from Virginia State University, both a Masters degree in Clinical Social Work as well as a Masters of Divinity degree from Howard University, and an earned Doctorate of Ministry degree in Prophetic Preaching for the 21st Century from United Theological Seminary.

Dr. Forbes, known as "The Change Architect", is a multi state licensed clinical therapist. She is the Founder and Chief Executive Officer of Khaalida Forbes Enterprises. This enterprise seeks to offer opportunities for transformation in the areas of mental, emotional, relational, and spiritual health.

Having worked with adults and adolescents for 25 years, Dr. Forbes has extensive experience treating various forms of emotional disturbance. Her therapeutic modality of choice is cognitive behavioral therapy, and her specialization is trauma therapy. Dr. Forbes has held leadership roles in various organizations geared toward emotional health advocacy, with an emphasis on reconciliation of families from various ethnic backgrounds. Her endeavors have taken her around the world (Italy, Egypt, Israel, London), and she trains quarterly throughout the year to ensure that she is on the cutting edge of what is occurring in the mental health, and faith field, across the country.

It is not often that you come across a therapist and leader that can weave the clinical, practical, and spiritual in a way that the well adjusted as well as the acutely traumatized client can identify with. Dr. Forbes does this with equal parts finesse and innate ability. She strives to empower people to believe that thru competent and compassionate therapy they can be healed, restored, and see significant lasting changes in their lives.

Printed in the USA
CPSIA information can be obtained
at www.ICGtesting.com
LVHW040744190923
758344LV00045B/16/J